MW00605941

Hope through Community

Words and Images
in Response to a Global Pandemic

Compiled by Cynthia Franca
& Cheryl Perreault

Hope *through* Community
Words and Images in Response to a Global Pandemic

Front cover photograph
Clear Pink Dawn – Hopkinton State Park © Tom Sloan
www.tomsloanphoto.com

Front and back cover design by Lisa Breslow Thompson
www.lisathompsongraphicdesign.com

Interior photos by Chelsea Bradway, Lynne Damianos, and Christine Strickland.

Library of Congress Control Number: 2020917716
ISBN: 9781941573334

Published by Damianos Publishing
Saxonville Mills
2 Central Street, Studio 152
Framingham, MA 01701 USA
www.damianospublishing.com

Produced through Silver Street Media by Bridgeport National Bindery,
Agawam, MA USA
First printed 2020

The proceeds from the sales of this book will benefit three charitable organizations assisting with local, national, and world hunger: Project Just Because, Feeding America, and Action Against Hunger.

To learn more about this project, please visit
www.hopkintonthroughpoetrybook.com

Contents

Acknowledgments

Hope through Community: Words and Images in Response to a Global Pandemic came together with the help and support of many, for which we are deeply grateful.

Thank you to the 72 participants selected for this anthology who responded to the call for the art of poetry and true stories. The submissions were all very powerful and also showed a unique and inspiring spectrum of perspectives and topics addressing the concept of hope.

Thank you to the photographers, Chelsea Bradway, Lynne Damianos, and Christine Strickland who contributed a number of "The Front Steps Project" photographs for this anthology project. What a spirited visual documentation of this time in history that has been captured by these three talented photographers!

Thank you to all of the people and families who posed with impressive spirit for these timely photos on their front steps or thereabouts and also offered their perspectives on having hope during challenging times and supporting their own communities.

Thank you to Tom Sloan for allowing us to use his breathtaking photograph *Clear Pink Dawn – Hopkinton State Park* for the front cover of this anthology, representing "Hope through Community."

Thank you to HCAM-TV for being our partner since the beginning, helping us to promote the project Words of Hope in our Hopkinton community and beyond, and keeping us strongly connected especially in these challenging times.

Thank you all of you for truly having honored the meaning of community.

Lastly, thank you to our own families and friends for their frequent assistance and support involving questions and polling on book titles, book covers preferences, editing and more! Thank you, dear ones, also for keeping us grounded, good-humored and for helping to sustain our own sense of hope for the duration of this special project.

Cynthia Franca & Cheryl Perreault

Preface

It was mid-March of 2020 when our country and communities began to go into "lockdown" and "quarantine." Admittedly we felt stunned when first hearing the news that the COVID-19 pandemic was hitting the United States and also the entire world. This sudden new reality required a lot of bracing of ourselves and our families and letting go of past ways of being and living for most people and making a new normal of daily life.

The news of pandemic and need to shelter-in-place was exacerbated by hearing the news of so many very sick people in ICUs, the grief of families who have faced loss due to the pandemic, the halting of many businesses, the subsequent economy and subsequent new poverty and hunger of many people, the division in politics, the facing of racial violence and systemic and structural racial inequity, the facing of so many injustices and viruses of our society and civilization in this time of pandemic.

So how do we face such a challenging time? How can we help to reinforce the feeling of resilience and encouragement among us in contrast to so much bad news during the COVID-19 pandemic?

Cynthia served as positive-minded catalyst soon after lockdown was declared in Massachusetts by anonymously delivering over 100 inspirational notes to the people in her neighborhood. Her action had immediate positive impact and response. This further inspired her to propose the possibility of creating a book offering "words of hope" from community members. She called upon Cheryl, her friend from "down-the-street" and frequent co-collaborator offering creative arts programs for community.

As a duo, we decided to take action as co-editors and, in April 2020, the project "Hopkinton & Beyond - Words of Hope that Connect Us in Challenging Times (aka Words of Hope)" was born. We put a call out for words of hope from those we know from local art centers, writers' circles and open mics, with the goal of connecting community and promoting resilience and uplift. We also sent invitations to submit on social media and newspapers putting a call out near and far to make submissions of poems and stories expressing what gives people hope during challenging times.

By the end of May, we had 120 responses and contributions which spanned a spectrum of people's thoughts, emotions and life experiences. Some wrote about hardship from loss or love, some addressed the pandemic. Some thought to other hard times in life that taught them about having hope. Some thought about the present moment in quarantine.

We not only heard from local people, but we heard from a few people around the world as well. We put the book together in only five months due to Cynthia's impressive driven nature, sense of professionalism and her deep desire and commitment to have the book finished by the end of this challenging, historical year of 2020.

The truth be told, as we went through the work of recruiting and compiling the submissions, editing the eventual manuscript, and selecting and including community photographs of local people in pandemic times, we were going through our own personal challenges.

We realized that while we were serving as editors, we were also everyday people in search of abstract things with no guarantee like faith and hope for our own challenged daily lives. We consequently found the real-life words of poems, stories and songs served to lift our spirits during the process of making this book. We realized while going through the unknown of pandemic times that we might face anything in this unpredictable year. Yet the words from this anthology reminded us that life can be very frightening and very hard, but that there can be balance restored by good moments too. Good moments like more time with family, the pleasure of little things in daily life, noticing beauty, being out in nature, social justice and solidarity and giving and receiving love.

Consequently, we have been uplifted and encouraged by our own endeavor to create a book of people's words of hope which helped to get us through this pandemic of 2020. We offer this book out beyond us to people of our communities near and far, having hope that these words and images collected during a hard time of world and civilization will offer some stories and songs and poems that might resonate, lift the spirit and help people to feel a little more connection, love, encouragement, and even joy.

This book also serves as a means of collective contribution and care to serve those in need specifically facing hunger in these hard times of 2020. As editors we felt particularly concerned about those with limited resources facing hunger during the pandemic times that we were hearing about on the news. We asked each participant if possible, to offer payment in advance to pay for a copy of the book in addition to a $10 fee toward publishing and printing fees. We noticed the amazing synergy in responses to this request where some people indicated at this time, they could not afford the payment while others sent in payment beyond their participant fee to help cover the fee for those in need.

We have told all contributors that once the book is published and printing/publishing fees are all paid, all proceeds earned from book sales would be divided and donated to three charities involved with addressing hunger including local food pantry Project Just Because, Feeding America and Action Against Hunger.

The way we look at it, all the writers of these poems, stories and songs in this book are contributing to the cause. The people who purchase the books are contributing to the cause and you the reader are a part of this chain by holding this book in your hands, by reading these words and sending a wish or intention of well-being and hope out to the people facing hardship or grief by keeping those in need in your own awareness.

May this book serve to hold, help uplift and inspire one another through this year of pandemic and through the ongoing ebb and flow of facing ongoing joys and sorrows throughout our life.

May we feel the deep roots of our humanity intertwined through the pages of this book as well as through our individual and interconnected journeys of this lifetime.

May this felt experience of connection through the community of our poems and stories help us to give and receive the gift of being human and having hope.

Introduction

As the COVID-19 pandemic began to radically change the way many of us around the globe think, act, interact, and dream about what's to come, it seemed like a good idea to explore people's concepts of hope through writing. This unprecedented time in history has been a challenging reality to say the least. There has been a spectrum of experiences faced by people in the U.S. and around the world ranging from those minimally affected, to those on the frontlines of local leadership, food/essential industry and all the doctors, nurses, and health care staff working hard to save lives. There have been so very many patients gasping for breath in the ICUs, including over 200,000 in the U.S. who, as of September 30th, 2020, have already died with no time or place set aside for their loss and the grief of their loved ones, which is really, all of our collective loss and grief.

In our own desire for seeking the possibility of uplift in these times we have been facing, we put a call out for collecting words of hope consisting of poetry, stories, and prose from people in and beyond our communities. The responses we received were diverse and powerful. We heard from many local poets and writers – from published poets to occasional and emerging writers – as well as from writers from across the globe, including Australia, South Africa, and someone from NASA who once had a poem sent to outer space.

This anthology also consists of photographs submitted by three photographers who participated in "The Front Steps Project" in various communities of Massachusetts. All people were photographed in front of their homes during the time of pandemic. Some were dressed in costume, some celebrated events like birthdays and weddings pandemic-style. Some held signs to raise their voices for equity, kindness to one another, and taking care of the planet.

What we discovered from this project is that there are as many different perspectives about what hope is, as there are differences in the lived experiences and stories of all people. Additionally, writings in this book address hope as it relates to themes including resilience, courage, spirituality, positivity, justice, connection to the natural world and wishes for a better post-pandemic world.

We, as editors, were emotionally touched and spiritually inspired as we read each submission. We learned from collecting and compiling the contributions that, when you ask people for their words of hope, the stories you get in return can look incredibly different, but all of them collectively can help guide us—can help to make us feel like we're not alone.

The words of hope collected in this anthology are not meant to form a navigational chart for facing hard times in the present pandemic or future years. Rather, we hope that they form a sort of tapestry of authentic, interconnected voices from people near and far who have something to share about their experiences of life and its challenges. United, these voices can serve as representation of the threads of our many communities which, when woven together, might provide inspiration for looking outside of ourselves, holding each other up, and looking ahead for better times to come.

Co-editors of Hope *through* Community: Words and Images in Response to a Global Pandemic
Cynthia Franca & Cheryl Perreault

Untitled

Victor Perton

Why did I submit my poem? I was taken by the wisdom and foresight of the request for submissions to reinforce optimism in the face of the pandemic and beyond.

Victor Perton is the Chief Optimism Officer at The Centre for Optimism based in Melbourne, Australia serving members in 54 countries. After serving globally as an adviser to the G20 presidency, before that a trade commissioner to the Americas and before that a parliamentarian and barrister, he was perplexed by negativity about leadership. His Eureka moment came in 2017, the leadership is OK but lost from sight in a fog of pessimism. Every day, Victor asks people "What makes you optimistic?" www.centreforoptimism.com

Untitled

The times call for realistic and infectiously optimistic leaders.
The leader is the person in your mirror.

© Chelsea Bradway

"The Front Steps Project was such a wonderful way for our community to come together, without actually 'coming together'. It was truly heartwarming to see what our small town was capable of when an opportunity presented itself."

~ Kimberly Laurie ~

Stop for a While

Patti Gurekian

I find inspiration for poems through family, travel, hiking, biking, cross-country skiing, singing, dancing, and reading about anything and everything.

Patti Gurekian is a retired Navy officer, educator, and mother of twins, who lives in Waltham, MA.

Stop for a While
(To the millennials in my life)

Share a beer with me

In lofty words
lift me
from this ground
that has found
too many
to bury;

Share a joke with me

In this short day
make me
laugh at the grief
that has swept
and kept
me away;

You are young
and your hours are long,

So stop for a while
and delight me;

Show me
how to dance
through my pain,

Show me
how to love
what remains.

Birthdays in the Time of Pandemic

Trisha Knudsen

Writing daily poetry has been a great release valve for all of the stresses of these first months of the year. This particular poem came from feeling frustrated at missing my grandchildren's birthdays. Stay well and healthy, friends – and keep moving forward. I'll see you on the other side!

Trisha Knudsen is a published poet, retired special needs teacher, professional editor and owner of RetreatQuest, offering creative arts and writing workshops and retreats for women. She has been writing poetry for 45 years. Trisha set herself a task to write a poem a day in 2020, and what a year it has been! She turned 60 in January, got a Bernese Mountain Dog puppy (now 6 months and 70 pounds!), it's an election year and we are all under quarantine for COVID-19!

Birthdays in the Time of Pandemic

My two grandsons are having birthdays this spring.
Little BIG Gus will be two on April 16th.
He doesn't know what day his birthday actually falls on,
so, it won't be too hard for him not to have a party with anyone
but his immediate family and his other grandma,
who's in quarantine with them.

His big brother Max, who will be five on May 22nd,
does know that he is turning five. He does know
the actual date of his birthday. He has been planning a
Fire Ninja party with his mom, and adding weekly items
to his party list of things to do and friends to invite
since his last birthday. He will be heartbroken to learn
that a party this year is not in his immediate future.

We will not be with them. We haven't been with them
for more than a month now, having sequestered ourselves
into our home an hour and a quarter away in another state.
We are grateful that the boys and their family, our family,
are healthy and safe and we are doing our part to keep them that way.

© Chelsea Bradway

"As we were looking for ways to connect to and help our community during this uncertain time, we were excited to learn that Southborough was participating in this beautiful initiative. We scheduled our photo for our son's first birthday to make this particular April day at home feel a little more festive than the rest; Chelsea turned our time on our front steps into a sweet and memorable cake-smash experience."

~ Sydney Lindstrom ~

But this virus has changed our lives as it has changed the lives
of everyone in the world. Insidious bastard virus.

It could be worse, I know. But it is damn hard to sit still
and miss the celebrating and the memorializing
and the plain everyday bits and pieces of life.
Like going to the grocery store without masks and gloves
or, as we are doing, ordering food and various necessities online
and bleaching everything that sits on the front stoop
once it has been delivered, then washing and drying every item
or removing it from its packaging to new packaging.
Then, of course, there is the washing of our hands
approximately a million times a day.

We will celebrate with Gus and Max by video chatting with them
from our living room on their special days. I have already sent
their gifts directly to their house for their mama to wrap and give them
from GahGah and Grandpa. I hope by the time our granddaughter Linnea's
birthday comes in October, we will all be together again, eating
cake and ice cream and hugging one another a little harder
and a little longer. May it be so that you too will soon be celebrating again.

Untitled

Norman Nichols

89 years above the grass. Norman Nichols retired in1994 from the mechanical engineering field, with music, pointed pen calligraphy, writing humorous poetry avocationally in the wings. Ready, with banjo, at a moment's notice to sit in with a trad jazz band.

His obit: He Came, He Went, Old What's His Name.

Untitled

I named her Felicia.
Her cat book description was Domestic Tabby.
She came to me, I don't remember how, only a couple
of weeks young. Thinking back, it may have been Beth and
Paul, my landlady and lord. They had a German Shepherd,
Teddie, and a place in Vermont and were into Morgan horses.

Felicia, that young, had her home in the bottom drawer of
the bureau in my one room apartment. I put a clock with
an audible tick/tock in, as the book said, to have a near-
comfort of a mother's heartbeat. She stayed in the drawer
while I was at work a short half-mile away. My landlord,
Paul, worked as a machinist there and was how I learned
about the apartment.

We had to move when the house was sold; the area is now
a mini-mall. Paul, Beth and Teddie moved to Vermont and
their Morgan's. Felicia and I moved to a second floor
apartment in Brighton. Nothing much to say about that.

A short stay at a hutch in the woods in Billerica before moving
again. Let out before the move, I lost her and had to return
a couple of times calling "psss, psss" and "kitty, kitty." From
somewhere she came 'meowing' right up to me and I picked
her up for a hug.

A small house on Heard pond in Wayland was our next venture and much adventure. The house was at the end of a dirt road with no other houses close by.

Whose book was it that said something to me that recalled the reprimand from my father for an interference I made to something my brother was doing. I can't remember the exact wording but this is close enough, 'let and help people you love be all that they can be.' I bring that up because I applied it to Felicia, now a full-grown cat, when, now out in the 'woods', she ventured outside to eat the grass and pheromone a tom.

Did I fear once outside she wouldn't return? Probably so, but stronger was the feeling that she should be everything she wanted to be. And if that meant being a more complete member of the wild, it was hers to do. She always returned and the door was always open...

And a new assignment, homes for all those kittens.

When the Summer Comes

John Boehmer

I believe each of us is born with powerful resources within us that we are taught to unlearn or deny. Much of the suffering we undergo is the product of our own mind. To possess hope is to become a child; a state in which everything becomes possible.

John Boehmer has been writing poetry, songs and composing music for most of his 63 years. He was born in New Orleans where he spent his early years and now lives in Andover Massachusetts with his wife Chris.

When the Summer Comes

When the summer comes
I'll be far away from here
Climbing on the roots and branches of a better year
Ah when the summer comes
I'll be sleeping safe and warm
Sheltered from the lash of this malign and violent storm
Secretly borne away
On a river flowing under me
When the summer comes

When the summer comes
I'll walk out through my back door
On to peaceful bird-loud roads I've never walked before
Ah when the summer comes
I'll be gazing at your star
Wishing for your love that shines on me from oh so far
To be tenderly brought to me
On a river flowing to my feet
When the summer comes

When the summer comes
I'll be lost without your love to show the way
When the summer comes
I'll be frightened of the night
And of the day

Ah when the summer comes
And you're arriving from your star
Even in my fear and trembling I'll know who you are
Ah when the summer comes
In the raiment of my dreams
Falling like a cloak of light until the brightness streams
Radiantly over me
Like a river flowing through the sun
When the summer comes
When the summer comes

© Lynne Damianos

"We participated in this project because it was a fun way to donate to an organization and take family photos during the COVID-19 pandemic. While practicing social distancing, with the help of Lynne, my family was able to create lasting memories during this unprecedented time through photos."

~ The Barrack-Anidi Family ~

124 Notes

Cynthia Franca

This story was written in the first days of quarantine, one day after the International Day of Happiness. They were the beginning seeds for the blooming of my wish to bring words of hope to the community and the world!

Cynthia Franca is author of a book of Brazilian poetry, Poetic Treasure, published in Brazil in 2003. She has lived in Hopkinton, MA for seven years. Author, local contributing artist/writer who has shared bi-lingual poetry, storytelling artist talks, and paintings at community arts events in Massachusetts. Coordinator, co-editor and poet of the Hopkinton 300th Anniversary Poetry Anthology Project; poet, juror and editor of Art on The Trails Southborough Project; co-director of the Creative Circles – Art for All! community art program; and coordinator with Cheryl Perreault of the Words of Hope Project, whose goal is to invite the community to submit poems and stories to promote community resilience and uplift, in response to the challenging time during the coronavirus pandemic.

124 Notes

Saturday, March 21, 2020. Early morning. I wore my disposable gloves and began my secret mission: spread happiness in my neighborhood. I have 124 notes in my pocket, printed in different bright colors. I will put them in all the mailboxes around me.

The roads were empty in total silence. Ghost town. A police car crosses the street. I hide the cards. Between the smiley face on the top and a heart in the bottom, the words in the note reveal my caring secret:

"Hi neighbor!

We're all stuck at home,
keeping our distance from others.
Doing our bit to keep our families and the world healthy.

Stay positive! Be strong!

We are all in this together!

Take care of yourself and your family!

Sending love and health,

Your neighbor"

In light of the coronavirus pandemic, the idea of sharing a note maybe can bring us together, as family and community, to focus on practicing gratitude, kindness, love, and compassion.

Later in that day, I saw a post on my neighborhood Facebook page:

"Thank you so much to the kind neighbor, whoever you are, who left this in the mailbox! It provided some much-needed cheer and encouragement! 😇*"*

If I made one person happy, that truly made my day.
Deep in my heart I just wanted to do something for people.

We are all in this together!

My Mother's Pandemic

Howard J. Kogan

Laughing at things that are no laughing matter is a kind of hope.

Howard J. Kogan is a retired psychotherapist and writer. His two books of poetry, *Indian Summer* and *A Chill in the Air* are available from the publisher, Square Circle Press or Amazon.

My Mother's Pandemic

It's a shame my mother missed a rare opportunity for
vindication and triumph by not living to see the coronavirus.
She always knew it was on its way, even precisely
where it was lurking, waiting to pounce –
on some public toilet seat, also known as a *strange toilet seat*
like one you might need to use at *God forbid,*
a place like Grand Central Station,
that pandemic playground she was certain
would erupt one day like Mt. Vesuvius
and make us into another Pompeii.

Frankly it wasn't much fun being infected by her fears
and yet now I must admit I see her in a different light,
no longer a neurotic germophobic nut,
but a pandemic prophetess wearing a hazmat suit
over her housedress, armed with alcohol wipes in one hand,
Lysol spray in the other, clucking self-righteously;
How many times did I tell you?
The coronavirus wouldn't have had a chance!

Sunshine Vision

Cathy Taylor

In these strange days of coronavirus, we need to remember nature as a vital force in our lives.

Cathy Taylor is a retired middle school teacher working creatively with words and art and an occasional song. She is a regular at open mics in the MetroWest and Worcester area including poetry events at Club Passim in Cambridge, as well as participating regularly at HCAM Studios in Hopkinton. www.cathyweavertaylor.com

Sunshine Vision

Watch for sunshine vision,
think Goddess,
smell forest,
dream.
Essential friend,
whisper moment,
be together. Soar!

When will hot summer fiddle juice
swim in lake water
and feel lazy, languid power
of pounding rain?
Take me like I am
singing beneath the storm.

Shadow woman asks about all,
but tells one essential truth.
Life is a luscious garden.
Share bounty,
eat fruit,
be gardener.
Live like true sky.
Always run through mist.
Transform from seed to fruit to seed once again.

To Lightning

Judith Ferrara

This poem is based on an incident told to me by a friend about her mother. It made me think about how we get through any harrowing experience and are permanently changed.

Judith Ferrara is a writer and visual artist who lives in Worcester, MA. Her poetry and essays have been published in three collections: *Gestures of Trees* (2000), *A Brush with Words* (2013) and *The Little O, the Earth: Travel Journals, Art & Poems* (2015), and in journals. Please visit www.PaletteAndPen.com to see her artwork and read the complete collection of Judy's Journals, a monthly blog about the creative process which she has written since 2004.

To Lightning

You spilled juice across the sky
No pas de deux of cloud and wind
No rampaging crescendo
Just a swift, breathtaking blast
Delivered while I waited out the storm
At my screen door

To fall backwards
Surprised thud of charged skin and bones
Dropped like a gift
At the feet of Zeus

To be hummed, beaten by your zing
Is one way to be divided and burned

For weeks afterward, under the air
Flavored with pink and orange waltzes
You administered a therapy of charms
Made me respect magic, darkness and the

Narrowness of my soul

Reprinted by permission of Judith Ferrara, *A Brush with Words*, Autumn Light Press, 2013.

© Lynne Damianos

"We joined The Front Steps Project to remember this unforgettable time in history, that we all been stuck at home during this pandemic. Participating in this project also gave us the opportunity to make a donation to continue to bring music, art exhibitions and events at the Amazing Things Arts Center."

~ The Castaneda Family ~

Hope in the Midst of a Worldwide Health Event: 2020 COVID-19 Virus

Geri Holland

I wrote this poem from my years of growing up in a city on the North Shore in the 1950's. It was a time of recovery for all our families, especially fathers, uncles, neighbors who served in World War II. Our neighbors, friends and family didn't have much, but we always found a way to help a neighbor when in need.

Geri is best known for working at Hopkinton Town Hall for over 30 years and dedicating her life to serve Hopkinton community with love, and honor. She is a local contributing artist, one of the founders of The Women's Art Forum (WAF) in 2007, and Co-director of the Creative Circles – Art for All Program in 2017.

Hope in the Midst of a Worldwide Health Event: 2020 COVID-19 Virus

When we are faced with challenging worldwide life events,
when we are separated from those we love,
when we accept our new reality,
we then begin to reflect on what truly matters,
that is, hope for our future.

We strive to have peace that passes all understanding of these events.
We push forward to keep our hope intact,
we have the strength to pass on unconditional love for one another...
Inspiring them to move forward knowing that we are all in this together.
We may be in isolation, but we are not alone.

Where Will You Go to See Him?

John Gaumond

When my sister's husband passed away, she asked me to write a poem for his funeral. My poem is meant to give comfort in the time of loss.

John Gaumond is a poet and photographer from Worcester, MA. His work has appeared in several journals, magazines and newspapers.

Where Will You Go to See Him?

No earthen prison will hold
him to a single place.
Instead his body and spirit
will be with nature
as he wished.

No separate stone
will note his passing.
Now each rock
along the trails he trod
will be a step to mark
his way of life.

In fields and woods
where he found
pleasure in the hunt.
Lakes, rivers, and ponds
offered him challenges
with rod and reel.

On the brightest day
or the darkest night,
seek not just to
find him there.

Look in places
where he will always be:
in your thoughts,
each pleasant memory,
and your hearts.

Forest of Community

Deana J. Tavares

I believe that our stories and perspectives unite us and remind us that we are not alone in this world, especially in times of distress. I wrote this story while thinking about my own community and then realized that it could reach out even further and may possibly bring a sense of hope to many.

Deana J. Tavares is a creatively fluid artist, poet, songwriter, activist, and actor. Growing up on the south coast of Massachusetts, many of life's hurdles only further strengthened her drive towards the arts. Her deep connection to the natural world and humanity is regularly reflected back through her visual artwork, poetry, and songwriting. As an avid writer and visual artist, her work leads her in various directions. Her latest explorations are currently in the direction of non-fiction.

Forest of Community

Just like any other major crisis that has taken place within the history of our world, the coronavirus is no different. We are all going through the ebb and flow of very trying times and riding upon the waves of uncertainty. For me, new questions are emerging daily. Where do we go from here? What has this strain on our economy and our hearts taught us? Has it strengthened our already established value systems? Or has it created awareness to try a new approach moving forward? What matters? Where are you within this very moment?

The sky has turned to grey and the rains have come once again, but there's always a rainbow in the clouds. There's a collective stillness in most of world right now, yet so much change is happening all around. We have been social distancing for quite some time, though we never used that term. Social distancing ourselves from our community by not sharing our stories, by not opening our minds and hearts to new ideas, by closing the doors to change, because change is difficult and scary at times. COVID-19 has taught us that change is inevitable and sometimes completely out of our control. It teaches us that all life is fragile, all lives matter, and every story should be heard while we are still here. I believe that currently we are seeing the intersection of humility and humanity converging in a symphony of voices. When crisis looms, our ears become fine-tuned to the notes of fear and desperation that hover all around. Sounds become more distinguishable because they are shared cries of discomfort and grief.

I see, hear it all, and have a deep appreciation for the kindness that is displayed every day. I believe that it is important for the mind, body, and spirit to hold onto joy and hope as much as possible. Small acts of kindness remind us that we are all deeply rooted here. Even though we are apart, our branches are still reaching out for one another. Let us all reap the benefits of this colorful palette of community and keep painting wide brush strokes across our towns long after the coronavirus has bid us adieu.

I have had various hurdles within my life that have heightened my awareness to the fragility of life. However, we are now experiencing a collective awareness regarding that very fragility. Hope and positivity have always pulled me through difficult times and this time has been no different. My hope for my community and the world as a whole is that we will all be able to see and hold onto the cracks of light shining through the darkness of these days. After the sadness, I wish you laughter. After the silence, I wish you fullness. After the fear, I wish you peace. After the uncertainty, I wish you positive changes. We can do better!

"Alone I am but one tree, but together we are a forest. " ~jummyjeenz

Untitled

Ron Whittle

Having lived through and survived the war in Vietnam and returning home with the residual effects of "Agent Orange", I have come to realize that "hope" is one of the few things in life that a price tag can't be put on.

Ron Whittle native son to the state of Massachusetts and Worcester, a Vietnam Veteran. A published poet of four books by Human Error Publishing from Greenfield, MA. Ron divides his writing time between Worcester and the shores of Cape Cod, where long beach walks provide inspiration and passion. Ron is currently co-host of a poetry show called the Poetorium at the Starlite Gallery and Lounge in Southbridge, MA and speaks all over New England.

Untitled

Tomorrow will always
look easier than today
It is in the nature of all things
Today we are bathed
in the light the Angels
bring to this fortuitous
morning
While tomorrow is still only
a gentle breeze of
happenstance at this
present moment in time
It is but a revelation of God's
probability of what
is yet to come
that opens new direction
and unexpected
paths to follow
in the serendipity of
all things godlike and holy

Like Them She's Gone into the Light

Terence Hegarty

My poem tries to express, in highly structured form, the sense that, although moral imperatives seem to have abandoned us in the real world, a mysterious and compelling sense of deep caring persists at the edges of our experience.

Dublin-born and bred Terence Hegarty is a songwriter and (occasionally) poet who lives in Holliston, MA. He has been active on the Boston area open mike scene since 1996.

Like them she's gone into the light, the light
that hides and comforts, far from madding crowds.
Yes, gone, I emphasize it. No one's night
can trace trajectories like hers through clouds
of knowing, then unknowing, to the lost
and bright lit harbor where she now resides
so distant from our dark. No one has crossed
that line but her. And yet her love abides
with us, its homely place. Our broken heart
achieves and strives, its purpose scarcely known.
She does not search the evil; it's her part
to care; she whispers that we're not alone.
So thick to think we'll ever understand.
Enough to know we touch her outstretched hand.

Fir in March

Polly Brown

Last year, I started sitting by the same window every morning, to write about what I saw. I had always loved the little fir tree, and it came to mean even more to me as I noticed how it was always different, through different lights and weathers, no two mornings exactly the same--and yet always itself. As the pandemic unfolded, that morning time, honoring the daily life of that one small tree, helped to steady me through dread and sorrow. And isn't that what hope is? The knowledge that on some scale, always, we can find ourselves in the presence of grace.

Polly Brown's most recent book, *Pebble Leaf Feather Knife*, from Cherry Grove, explores the natural world, what it means to us, and how we fit in it. She's a member of Every Other Thursday, a group of Boston area poets. She has written about war and peace with the help of mentors at the Joiner Institute for the Study of War and Social Consequences at UMass Boston, and on her own Hopkinton hillside, where she has lived for 38 years, she has helped organize outdoor poetry readings on the Center Trail.

Fir in March

Years ago I reached a string
of lights for Christmas to the top
on this tree now twice my height.

Birds sleep through storms there
under an evergreen cloak:
small needles woven

so dense no hawk can enter.
(Even a strong wind sets the tree
atremble only gently.)

Now a sparrow heads in,
nest fodder scribbled in her beak,
Almost I remember

breaking from an egg
deep in that shadow,
climbing to light.

© Lynne Damianos

"We participated in this project because we love our front porch! It's the best room in the house. From its steps and porch swing, we see and greet all our neighbors. And of course, because we love Lynne! Any project she chooses to take on is one we would also support."

~ The Reitzes ~

Could There Be Spring?

Bonnie Perkel

This poem was written on a surreal snowy day in mid-April (2020) when COVID-19 was a frightening new reality, and surging in Massachusetts, causing us to stay at home. The virus seemed as surreal as the spring snow outside, but I was reminded that this was a snapshot in time and life would go on. There was hope in the fact that nature, and the mundane, would prevail.

Bonnie has spent many years working in the field of education as a teacher, student advisor, and college administrator. She is also a writer/editor who holds a master's degree in the Waldorf method of education. Bonnie recently migrated back north to Massachusetts after a 12-year stint at Duke University in North Carolina.

Could There Be Spring?

April 18 and light cotton balls of snow
fall on daffodils, while confused
budding trees stand alone
and clear eyes peer from quarantined
windows. We know
the snow will soon melt. The dull buds
will burst into moist pink blossoms before
green leaves appear.
And we might not see it happen unless
we stay behind the glass, watching.
Not touching. Blessing every sacred breath.

© Lynne Damianos

"Lynne has been proactively involved with the Framingham community for a long time. When I saw her Front Steps Project, I was eager to participate; it seemed so positive and uplifting. I booked the appointment for Earth Day to celebrate the planet."

~ **Kathy Swift (aka Nana) and Madeleine Swift** ~
(aka Favorite Granddaughter, aka Only Granddaughter)

Let's Rewrite Our Human Story

Jan Krause Greene

I wrote this story because I believe we are intimately connected, not only to each other, but also to all life on earth.

Jan Krause Greene, a former high school teacher and newspaper columnist, is the author of *I Call Myself Earth Girl*. She uses fiction and poetry to examine the human spirit in face of good times and bad. *What Happens in the Space between?* a cross-genre work of eco-fiction with a mystical twist will be released in 2021. www.jkgreene.com

Let's Rewrite Our Human Story

In the midst of the difficult challenges and the grief many of us feel because of COVID-19, I am wondering if humanity can rewrite the stories we have told ourselves about what it means to live on this planet.

Our rewritten story must begin with a new way of knowing. A knowing that has been buried in our psyches, a knowing that is waiting to burst forth from our battered hearts and fragile spirits, a knowing that reminds us how very important we are because we live at *this* very moment in history. All of us who live on earth now are living in the space between what was and what will be. Of course, this could be said of every generation. But *this* space, *our* space in time, may be the most important transitional moment in human history.

Our new story must begin with our connection to all life on Earth. We exist as part of a complex web of symbiosis and parasitism, of competition and collaboration, and in human history, of domination and subordination. Humans have often acted in ways that are out of balance with the natural order. We have often been parasites, living off the natural world, taking from nature, but not helping it regenerate. We have competed, more often than collaborated. We have believed we can dominate the natural world and each other. Now, we are learning that this way of life is diminishing humanity's chances of survival. Our mistake has been not recognizing our inextricable connection to the natural world, to the ecosystems that sustain us, and to all humans.

Our new story tells us we have an unprecedented opportunity to change the way we live for the better and to raise the standard of living for those who have been underserved. We, who live now, have been chosen by God, or the universe, or random chance to create a better world. I believe we can. We will invent, adapt, and cooperate in order to survive. We don't have to accept that some must always live in poverty. We don't have to accept that displaced workers will be forever unemployed and unappreciated. We don't have to accept that politics will keep us forever divided and angry. We can use this existential crisis as an opportunity to create a better world.

The point is this. Our new story is one of hope because as individuals and as societies we can learn to live in harmony with nature and with each other. None of us will ever make the whole difference; none of us can change the world. Each of us must find our role in making changes, big and small, that bring more love, more justice, more joy into the world. The power of one, really means the power of each one to do our part. How very valuable each of us is. Because what happens next is up to *all* of us!

A Good Day

Virginia Nigloschy

I wrote this poem because I have found in my life that "acceptance" has been the answer to my life's challenges. The day I wrote this poem started out to be a hard day as we were six weeks into the COVID-19 lockdown. Imagining what it would be like to practice acceptance of the pandemic lockdown, I was inspired and then had an experience of acceptance... wrote about the experience and then had a "Good Day."

Virginia Nigloschy is a mother of four children. She has been writing as well as feeding and caring for people for most of her life. She writes primarily to understand herself, other people and the world she lives in.

A Good Day

Daylight has come. The night has given way to a new day and the practice of acceptance begins. To let be what is. Or, is it to be what is? An opportunity to be a human being not a human doing. Who are we really? Where are we going? Why so restless and on the move? There is something rich and full right here to satisfy my restlessness. I sense it deep within me. I need not earn, achieve or search for it. It is beyond my naming. I cannot capture it, it captures me. Although, somehow we mutually agree. It is elusive and cannot be held in my hands for long. It flies from my grasp like a free bird in the wild, setting me free to be, even if only briefly. Freedom is found in contentment as I sit here with my cup of coffee, in the silence of my living room, sun streaming in the window behind me, crackling noises from my baseboards as the heat comes on intermittently breaking the silence. Everything I am and have are right now. What I have is my life, warmth and a cup of coffee. And they are all gifts given to me as an entrance way to the miracle of being and being fully alive to all that is and is all in this moment. I am grateful and complete.

© Chelsea Bradway

"Our community is like an extended family; we can't imagine going through life without them."

~ **Laure Keough** ~

To Aiden

Tom Smith

Bringing a child into the world is perhaps the greatest expression of selflessness, sacrifice, and hope. In a world of great uncertainty, this hope may be shrouded in questions, doubts and fear. I addressed this poem to my grandson on the day he was born, but the real audience was his parents.

With four studio albums to his credit, Tom Smith is best known as a performing songwriter with frequent appearances at folk festivals, coffeehouses, libraries and church basements. His popular monthly blog "The Kitchen Musician" (www.tomsmithmusic.com) features newly written songs and Tom's reflections on living in the modern world.

To Aiden
(For Aiden Paul Smith
On the occasion of his birth, March 29, 2018)

Today for the first time
you rest on the outside of the familiar body that nurtured you from a seed,
from a wish,
from a hope,
from a promise.
It was a long and difficult journey, but now you are home.

Home is a mother and a father who love you since before there was light,
before there was breath,
before the sound of your trumpet cry to announce that you claim your place
among humankind.

They have much to teach you
and they have much to learn from you.

May the blessings of this day
the wish of this day
the hope of this day
the promise of this day
the love of this day
be reborn for you each and every day of your life.

Pebble

Christiana Boehmer

Pebble presents one of the messages that Chris finds most useful in this moment. When we feel keenly the smallness of our acts of hope or defiance, we should also remember the large impact that a small act can have, and take heart.

Christiana Boehmer is a songwriter from Andover Massachusetts. She's been writing songs since she was five. Writing songs helps her work through feelings, explore ideas, craft funny stories, deliver the sermons she needs, and find the kernel of truth in dreams.

Pebble

Pebble on the shore seems like nothing
Pebble in a shoe makes a grown man stop
Pebble in a pond makes a ripple
Shake a pail of sand and the pebble's on top
Itty bitty tiny little nothing
Itty bitty tiny little thing
Never underestimate the impact
Of an itty bitty tiny little…tiny little thing

Penny in the street seems like nothing
Penny in your pocket and you feel okay
Penny for your thoughts tells a story
Toss it in the air, it'll go your way
Itty bitty tiny little nothing
Itty bitty tiny little thing
Never underestimate the impact
Of an itty bitty tiny little…tiny little thing

Every little pause in the music
Every little lift of the artist's pen
Every little nod from a stranger
Every little word from a distant friend
Itty bitty tiny little nothing
Itty bitty tiny little thing

Never underestimate the impact
Of an itty bitty tiny little...tiny little thing

Spring Watch

Barbara Feehrer

The comforting cycle of the seasons and the special joy of spring after our long NE winters inspired my poem about spring peepers. In this pandemic season, I was especially excited about the return of spring. Hearing those little peepers this year was really a sign of hope and promise.

Barbara Feehrer is a retired educator who has lived and taught in Bedford for many years. Graduate of Tufts University (BA) and Boston College (MEd). Mother of two, grandmother of seven young adults. After her retirement she has enjoyed studying and writing poetry and finds her greatest inspiration in nature. She is a member of two poetry workshops in Concord and Carlisle, and has published in several journals and anthologies, and also published a collection of her work titled *Lake Lessons: Reflections.*

Spring Watch

It's April again, and I am waiting...
listening for the sound, the joy
of spring peeper trills
Will it be tonight?

This morning, across the road
where the neighbor's yard slopes
to the spring-swollen Concord River,
rough tree trunks rise from dark water.
Early mists drift among bare branches.
The moment deeply quiet,
the water cold and still.

April's afternoon sun
gently warms the earth.
The water responds...
begins to pulse and move,
ready for the great event.

Tonight the pools come alive,
the singing starts, the chorus builds.
Life bubbles up in the essence of the season.
Clear sounds, sweeter than a favorite symphony
ring out in the waiting night.

Listen! It's spring! The peepers are here...

dorothy...

Jamele Adams

I wrote the poem out of the pain of loss and share it for the love I hope it inspires.

Jamele Adams (also known as Harlym1Two5) remains well known nationally and is a frequent and highly regarded figure in competitions, performance, concert and beyond. He has also become well known in the Boston area for leading workshops dealing with issues of diversity, equity and inclusion. Jamele is often asked to be a panelist or to give presentations on a broad range of topics regarding diversity and pluralism, and also is asked to prepare presentations in response to very specific incidents or conditions. Appearing at dozens of college campuses every year. He is the "HUMAN HIGHLIGHT OF POETRY AND EDU-ACTIVISM."

dorothy...

COVID-19 got our grandmother
They said no one could visit her
Couldn't sing through the windows cause she can't stand
They said she too weak to hold the telephone
Every time we call
It takes 30 minutes to hear her breathe
Because they have to find someone available to suit up
And hold the phone for her
They said she just mumbles now
Only able to say "I Love You"
It's happening so fast
Faster than her son who abandoned me
Faster than the person that blind-dated her to COVID-19
Faster than ventilators can arrive
Faster than breath

COVID-19 took grandma on Wednesday

With nanna til death
my cousin;
backwards

Upside down
Outside herself
Incapable

She's in New York,
Westchester county
New Rochelle
They said you shouldn't come to the state
They said we can't have a funeral

Our last words were
I love you
I'm not done
With them being done with her
How do you tell death its wrong

Nothing makes you
Want to be closer to someone
Than the invisible keeping you apart
Explain God to me

Answer the "question-less"
I don't know what to ask
But I feel like a question

The question mark of me
Is her exclamation point

Is this thing in heaven
Or does it stay with her body
Can her angel wings breathe

Does she have her voice back
and syllable
and strength
to speak to me
or does another angel have to hold my voice to her ear
to hear
I love you grandma.

Life Requires Us to Do the Impossible

Denise Moyo

While this poem talks about the impossible being required of us, it starts by saying it will happen again. In other words, what we think is impossible has been overcome before. This poem is actually about hope, and the expectation that life has for us to survive what we think is impossible to survive. It is possible to survive this, to overcome this, whatever the this is. That's the message this poem seeks to pass on.

Denise Moyo was born in Zimbabwe. She graduated from Boston University and is a licensed clinical social worker and licensed applied behavior analyst. Denise Moyo uses poetry and music to speak about God, issues of trauma and emotional pain, as well as many other different topics. Her poetry is presented in a way that is prayerful, transformative and healing. https://denisemoyo.com

Life Requires Us to Do the Impossible

It'll happen again.
Yes, in this day and age.
Life continues to require us to do the impossible.
We often find ourselves in circumstances
we would never have chosen.

In fact, there are people everywhere tonight,
aching for a different reality,
much like we do and our parents did.

There are some today,
sleeping on pavements in the cold,
in the rain.
And there are those who are marching
down the streets of loss
alone…all alone.

Challenges are meant to affect us,
to change us, but not destroy us.
Life is a mystery in that way.
It gives us storms

while cheering us on to survive.

As long as we remain alive,
it's just a matter of time.
It'll happen again.
The impossible will be required.

Reprinted by permission of Denise Moyo, *No Longer Prodigal: A Collection of Poetry*, CreateSpace Independent Publishing Platform, 2018.

Untitled

Owen Fitzpatrick

There is no doubt in my mind that my Mom will beat cancer. She will win.

Owen Fitzpatrick is a sophomore at Hopkinton High School and a member of the Cross Country, Winter and Spring Track teams. He is the founder of Running UP!, an innovative 5K training program that empowers kids, one step at a time.

Untitled

The first couple days after I learned my Mom had cancer still sting my memory. I remember sitting in my bed alone, thinking about her and how she could be gone forever. She couldn't hold cold things, she was always in pain, and her hands were full of blisters. My Mom had beautiful, long, curly hair and I watched it slowly fall out because of the chemo treatment. Hollow holes sat where her smile once lit up her face. Inside, I was slowly crumbling. I realized that I had to pull myself together, but when you find yourself in a situation like this, knowing where to reach and what to hold on to isn't easy. I first thought about all the reasons why I shouldn't be worried. For example, "My Mom is really tough" or "We caught it early." The trouble is, despite the fact that she's really tough, they didn't catch it early. She had no signs that the cancer was growing inside of her for years because she looks so healthy. Guilt swam in my head for weeks whenever I began to forget the grief I was feeling. Distraction is, essentially, forgetting grief. My Mom was in the middle of treatment when the quarantine quieted the world and the presence of her cancer rang louder and louder in my ears. I could Zoom and Xbox all I wanted, but there was no sunshine under the cloud of cancer that darkened our house.

I looked for hope in the darkness, but it didn't find me, and I didn't find it. Gifts flooded our house covered in the word hope. Hope. It became my least favorite word. I didn't want to hear hope or see hope. I do not hope that my mom beats cancer. She WILL beat cancer. She is defying every odd. She's running miles on the treadmill as soon as they draw that chemo infusion line out of her port. She's lifting weights and eating kale. She drove herself to chemo-radiation every single day for six weeks until she needed a wheelchair. When the doctors tell her maybe, she says, YES, I CAN. She will win. Hope is an excuse. Hope is a desire, and its fluffy-unicorn sense of maybe has no place for those needing action. Cancer isn't about hope. Hope floats. To those preaching hope, I say, find your fight and free your faith.

Mom, you've got this. I know it. I love you more than words.

© Chelsea Bradway

"We had the dress and a tux (both *sort of* fit), two adorable best people at our side, and the help of a professional photographer with an amazing vision to support local charities while making some fun memories during this surreal time. We had some fun with the selfies before Chelsea Bradway came to take the picture of our entire family outside. Thank you for indulging our silliness. Friends ... be well and happy and safe and kind."

~ Chris, Eva and Owen Lee and Beth Farry ~

Epithalamion

Terry S. Johnson

My reason for this poem: my daughter and now son-in-law decided to keep their planned wedding date as an act of confidence for the future, which is always unknown.

Terry S. Johnson served as a public school teacher for over twenty years. She loves to study languages, art, architecture, history and the movies. Her two poetry collections include *Coalescence* (New England Book Festival Honorable Mention 2014) and *Plunge* (2019).

Epithalamion

Coastal New England June
day, high tide and clear
after a fog-thick morning.
Long abandoned the ancient
Greek preference for a January
wedding, full moon rising.

Without invoking the Goddess
Hera or any god at all,
a daughter pivots from her parents
to her future, vows exchanged.

Those in attendance contemplate
their lives, tsunami of memory.
Weddings, births, degrees, jobs,
divorce. Or perhaps disappointment
in never having been chosen,
or joyous images of travel past,
a plague now hovering.

Distant thunder, darkening sky.
Just enough time for photos
before the predicted deluge.
The small gathering savors

their time together inside. As
guests depart, a strawberry moon
ascends between dissipating clouds.

Panhandler

Ken Slaughter

I wrote this poem before the coronavirus pandemic. The poem is one of several of mine that explore compassion, and some of the obstacles that get in the way of our better natures.

In 2011 Ken Slaughter came to the realization that most of his poems tend to be brief. He began searching for a short poetry form and discovered Tanka. Most of his poems are written in that form. For two years he served as vice president of the Tanka Society of America.

Panhandler

A tiny cynic
sits on my shoulder,
whispers in my ear,
laughs as I reach for my wallet.

What does he know?
His only friend is fear.

Crumbs

Malcolm F. Davidson

The reason I submitted this poem is because "crumbs, that will soon be a loaf of literature." All of us have crumbs of ideas, odd bits of creativity that need to be honored, need to be shared, need to be connected. Both within ourselves and with each other. It is not the crummy ideas of the business leaders or politicians that we need to look to for sustenance, but within our own minds, hearts and spirits, there lie the cakes, the loaves, whatever we wish to call it, but there it is for sure. On that we can trust, on that we can rely upon.

Malcolm F. Davidson is a 60's Boomer who worked in technology all of his career. He worked for Sony Music for many years and during that time began to develop the musical "Company Matters". He is a published poet and has performed at numerous locations in New England and Texas over the years. He has an honors degree in electrical engineering and a Masters in Computer Science, making a technology company a perfect fit for the Company Matters story arc.
www.companymatters-themusical.com

Crumbs

I am a maker of crumbs
I am a crumb maker, just ask my wife
The toaster is a veritable bounty
a crumb maker also, gorging on the bread
I feed it, carved from a loaf of good crusty Italian
olive oil, rosemary, whole wheat, they each offer
up crumbs of all hues and sizes.

I am a maker of crumbs, in the bedroom
crumbs of boxer shorts, odd socks
shorts, lying around from last summer
a shoe crumb, a slipper crumb, usually in pairs
but, nothing is beyond me the crumb maker.

My office is filled with crumbs of papers
for I am a crumb maker
old bills, half finished, crummy poems,
new poems that turn into old soon enough

books left to be read and now piled high
crumbs, that will soon be a loaf of literature.

I dare not mention the garage or the yard
crumbs of trees, sticks, logs, branches
all needing to be picked up
for I am a maker of crumbs.

The mind also contains crumbs
thoughts that drift in and out
ideas that hang around for a while
not crumbs, more the flour and yeast of something
part of the dream, the next big thing.

My wife has stopped cleaning up after me
The clothes sit on the chair and now and again
I'll scurry and put away, the socks and the shoes
Now, I'll scoop up the crumbs by the toaster
leaving it clean, but I look around the living room
and there are often crumbs of cups
thankfully not all mine
for we have a stream of people dropping by
leaving their own crumbs
towels, and coats, the odd umbrella
Tee shirts.

I love our crummy house and I love my crummy life.

"I wanted to be seen demonstrating perseverance, creativity, and positive energy in these uncertain times."

~ Patrick Steele ~

Reservoir of Light

Wendy Santis

"Reservoir of Light" is a poem I wrote inspired by my friend Malka Kutnick's (http://www.malkakutnick.com) painting of a southwestern cloudscape. Nature offers inspiration and relief during this pandemic.

Wendy Santis is a global health practitioner, singer and poet who grew up in Concord, MA and lives in Silver Spring, MD. She has done international development work in over 20 countries.

Reservoir of Light
inspired by Malka Kutnick's painting by the same name

A southwestern cloudscape at the edge of town,
floating magically, high above ground.
Release the darkness and look within
to these sacred contours, where my canvas begins.
My paintbrush has a mind of its own—
to capture nature's wonders and the great unknown.
It follows form and thought and takes its cue—
the mystery of clouds, this glorious view.
Morning light, an ethereal glow,
a dreamy sea of color, contrast and flow.
Textured waveforms on display.
Movement in time, lines and shapes at play.
An indigo palette for my artist's eye—
a reservoir of light in the churning sky.

Wait Until Later

Trish Perry

I wrote this poem shortly after the lockdown went into effect. At home, no place to go, my garden became the immediate focus of all my thwarted energy. Grand visions grew daily, but it turned out that the reality was harder to achieve – online viewing just didn't cut it (so to speak). I needed to see, touch, smell, but couldn't. The poem was my effort to turn frustration into humor!

Trish Perry has worked as psychologist, coach and consultant, dipping into poetry here and there. She and her husband, Fin, have lived in Hopkinton for 48 years.

Wait Until Later

Sun's out
Garden's cleaned up
Go.

I could:

Start seeds…OK. Get info online.
Indoors? Outdoors?
Need seeds and starter kits for indoors.
Maybe I'll buy little plants instead.
No seedlings available yet.
Wait until later.

Stake the peonies
(Discard the jury-rigged
cage from last year.)
Check out better methods online.
"Umbrella spoke"?
Chicken wire?
No materials here.
Wait until later.

Dig out the spreaders,
Solomon's Seal, Bee Balm, Coreopsis.
Lots of room now for new plants.
Check out open garden centers online.
Too many choices.
Need to see them in person.
Wait until later.

Side of house.
Dead witch hazel,
Scraggly vinca.
Should get soil tested.
UMass testing agri labs online say:
Not doing soil analysis now.
Wait until later.

Need to find out exactly when "later" is.
Check it out online.
Too many answers.
Guess I'll have to wait…until later.

Kindness: A Way of Living

Leone Carneiro Santos

I decided to share my story because I wish to share with others some ideas of what we can do to live in a better world as a community.

Leone Carneiro Santos is from Brazil. She is married and has a 14-year-old daughter. She considers herself a good-humored person who loves people, loves to help others, and loves to see people being happy. For hobbies, she loves to read, study, and travel.

Kindness: A Way of Living

I am Leone and I live in Brasília, Brazil. I would like to share with you some actions I have done in these pandemic´ times. I believe in helping people. One of my life´s missions is helping others. Sometimes, I ask myself: in what ways can I connect with other people to see that I can make a difference to them?

We are living in a time of challenges and uncertainties. In March, our routine was completely looped. Suddenly, I can't meet my neighbors and friends. So, my family decided to keep in touch with them in different ways. In the beginning of March, we did a collage with words of hope, peace, faith, love, and put them in the six elevators of my building. I received feedback from some of my neighbors who thanked us.

I also decided to call a friend each day only to ask how they are doing and if they need something. One of my close friends told me her daughter had a fever and needed some medicine. She was alone with her children and asked me to buy the medicine. Of course, I did. It is amazing to have the opportunity to help others.

My friends know that I love sweets with coffee. One of my friends, Karla gave me a piece of banana bread. After that, a group of colleagues shared foods with one another. I love canjica*, a Brazilian typical food. A neighbor in my condo residence found out and cooked and shared canjica with us. It was amazing.

It has been common here to celebrate birthdays from our front doors. My friend Marcela completed 33 years. To celebrate, some colleagues went to sing birthday songs for her in front of her door. We also brought a birthday cake.

For me, helping and being kind are a way of living better by making a difference in my community and to live with purpose.

* Canjica is a Brazilian sweet dish, associated with winter festivals, which in Brazil is in June. The dish is a porridge made with white de-germed whole maize kernels, cooked with milk, sugar and cinnamon until tender.

Sea Inside

Ginger Gibeault

These past months have had a sadly narrowing and sometimes crippling effect on our lives, but if we look, REALLY look, we might see the "One who is limitless ... and a love that encompasses like an ocean." This is my source of hope and inspiration that I would like to share with you.

To Ginger Gibeault, poetry is painting with words what we see. She has written poetry from the time she noticed the colors of the sky through her picture taking years discovering shadows and light. Until now ... a witness to such unfathomable sorrow together with an outpouring of compassion and community.

Sea Inside

Today is one of those days
when from the moment I wake up
I feel a strong yet undefinable yearning.
So I ask myself ...
What do I need to do today?
Where shall I go to soothe this desire?
The answer lies in the rhythm of the tides
In the unevenness of creeping white foam.

But today, like most days now, I cannot go there
To carve myself a seat in the sand
To open my eyes to the beauty of existence
then close them just to listen.
Maybe take a walk
feeling the grains of time between my toes.
To get my feet wet
and look for perfectly flat skipping stones.
To swim, ah yes, to swim!

No, not today ...
Instead, I will visit the sea inside.

Marathon Courage

Buck Locke

My wife Judy and I have volunteered at the hydration station 10 for the Boston Marathon for about ten years. Really impressed by the courage of the runners and those in wheelchairs, and some pushing those in wheelchairs, this poem reflects some of the emotion and hope the runners inspire.

Buck Locke is a retired engineer from Hewlett Packard Medical Products group. He enjoys writing poetry and meeting with those that enjoy poetry.

Marathon Courage

Can you visualize courage?
Look at the woman with a blade
With a missing foot to engage
The marathon she's not afraid

See the man with no legs
Straining with all his might
All pride, for nothing he begs
To push his wheelchair his right

For the embodiment of love
A father pushing a wheelchair
Son lying down looking above
Together they go disdaining despair

The winners are on the nightly TV
Runners strong setting records
Blessed beautiful bodies we see
Crowned with accolades and awards

But the wounded and disabled demonstrate
Courage made visible for they do the marathon
Not to set records that are great
But to go the distance means they have won!

I wipe a tear from my eye
Such courage makes me cry!
They keep HOPE alive
Their courage teaches all to thrive!

* Editors' note: The Boston Marathon was canceled for the first time in its 124-year history due to the COVID-19 pandemic. The annual race was held virtually in September 2020.

Corona Haiku

Robert W. Foster

I am an optimist and fully expect us to come out of this pandemic - but not soon. My generation started out in the Great Depression, grew up during World War II, experienced the atomic bomb and all its horrors, and the Cold War with all its dangers, followed by the Korean and Vietnam wars and various scurmishes and recessions ... so we are accustomed to global crises. In the midst of all this, I have found writing haiku serves as an emotional outlet and source of self-amusement.

Robert W. Foster is a widowed and retired civil engineer in his 80s. Writing and travel is what he likes best to do - when conditions allow. Robert is also the author of a small novel, *Michael's Eyes*, about the blind man in the Gospel of John who received his sight. In consideration of this story, Robert wondered how such a man could make his way in the world ... so he explored the possibilities.

Corona Haiku

A *scary* springtime;
home alone, but not lonely.
Nor COVID-19.

Sneeze in my elbow,
wash both my hands, *stay at home*.
survive the Virus.

Objects rare and strange:
meds, masks and breathing machines.
Hope, love, Skype and Zoom.

No sickness will last;
fever comes and goes away,
while the world spins on.

A *pretty* springtime:
sunshine, walks, some daffodils.
Friends and fam'ly still alive!

© Christine Strickland Photography

"We wanted to participate in The Front Steps Project to give back to others in the community through Project Just Because. It was a great way to capture this unique moment in time as a family."

~ **The Fitzpatrick Family** ~

Ode to the Locked-down Life

Anne Mattina

The poem recounts the monotonous repetition of our lives under lockdown using the situation's own absurdity to draw a smile from the reader. Out of the monotony emerges a ray of hope.

Anne Mattina is a Massachusetts native who has lived in Hopkinton with her husband and son for over two decades. She is a professor and chair of the Communication department at Stonehill College and is an active member of the Hopkinton Historical Society.

Ode to the Locked-down Life

most days the world is less than a 1/2 mile wide
awake, the dogs await their 2 block walk
promises of longer, farther, whispered
as they resist return
breakfast, headlines, email, texts
zoom: committees, classes, advisees,
camera on or off? sigh.
everybody please MUTE YOUR MICS
lunch
skyping with doctor, routine
rummage through frig & cabinets
hoping for dinner inspiration
none.
sanitizing wipes, gloves (2 pair, just in case) mask
ready.
follow the arrow in the grocery store
locking eyes above masks with scofflaws & rebels who wander their own
path
glaring murderously at those within personal distance
reaching up, over
"stay in your lane" takes on a whole new meaning here.
voices echoing above the near-empty meat case
looking in gloved desperation at thin plastic produce bags

it'll never happen.
toss fresh vegetables in the cart.
stand on painted footprints, 6-feet intervals from cashier
wait until belt is emptied & wiped, cashier beckons
unload groceries
enunciating every word thru mask & plexiglass
hand signs win out
return home
dogs
one is dancing
the other's nose diving straight into the grocery bags.
wipe down bottles, cans, boxes and jars
soak produce in vinegar & water
uninspired dinner prepared
eaten, cleared, cleaned.
time for promises kept
longer, farther
all the way around the big block this time.

Bitter to Sweet

Ron Israel

Bitter to Sweet is a song about how your attitude towards life can change when you see something dark and negative turn into something hopeful and uplifting.

Ron Israel is a singer-songwriter who puts great emphasis on lyrics. His songs are about love, life, and the times we live in. The lyrics in many of his songs can be interpreted in stand-alone spoken word presentations.

Bitter to Sweet

Put some sugar in my coffee
Plant a kiss on my cheek
Let me see the possibility
Of turning bitter to sweet

Take the man out of his blue song
Give him a different beat
Shifting grooves can mean a move
From bitter to sweet

That's what I love about you Momma
Your million different ways
Of taking on what seems to be lost and lonely days

Put a wink onto my black eye
Pour rosewater on my feet
Post a rainbow on the dark sky
Turn bitter to sweet

Cause playing in this big tent
You get wins and defeats
But there is magic in the moment
You turn bitter to sweet

That's why the only kind of hero
In this unnerving place
Is someone who can give our brew a different kind of taste

Now you may be full of anger
Take what happened and hit delete
But change your mind when you find
Bitter turn to sweet-bitter turn to sweet-bitter turn to sweet

What Doesn't Kill You Makes You Strong

June-Ruth A. Canonico

Reason for this particular story of Hope: My reflection on the most significantly terrifying experience in my teens aided my return to discover how I managed to find hope in that crisis then and years later. My family, friends and faith were the underpinnings of finding light and hope for a recovery then and now.

June-Ruth A. Canonico was raised in a family where storytelling, singing and humor were as integral as a life based around a Church community. Her being the only girl in a family of three brothers led her to find solace and wonder in reading Folk and Fairy Tales in the welcome shade of the willow tree her father planted outside her bedroom window. Tales that teach courage in adversity, hope in the dark woods, and joy in reunions and love were, and are, the bedrock of her life even now. Her "Twice Upon a Time: Tunefully Told Tales" program, formed in England in her 30's and 40's, continued in her return to the States 26 years ago and offers to those she shares these tales and songs, a door into the vitality of their own personal life stories.

What Doesn't Kill You Makes You Strong

As we move into week eleven of the lockdown of the pandemic, I, like many others, feel the sense of unreality as so much of our lives has been put on hold. We still do not know how long this paralysis of our daily lives will be halted by the need to stay sequestered. We hope for our lives to resume some semblance of normality in the near future, but we cannot know how long this will take.

I am of an age and with such medical conditions as to have made me more restricted in my movements than most, added to which I live alone.

There is no one to share my experience with day to day, face to face, hand to hand, voice to voice. How do I manage to sustain my sanity? For one, I have lived more and more in an unsolicited solitude for almost two decades. My mobility handicaps have restricted me from the work I love, teaching music to young children in schools. As my painful encroaching arthritis has taken hold of most of my weight bearing joints, my back and my hands and shoulders, I have been less able to even attend the concerts, Open Mics and events I so enjoy.

Ah, now, but where is the Hope in this story? Where is the inspiration of how I am managing this isolation?

Let me take you back to an evening 57 years ago in October. This was my sophomore year in High School. It was an exciting time of growing up and exerting my independence, albeit with resistance from my good yet conservative but loving parents. On that night, as five young people returned home from a youth roller skating party, driven by a 19-year-old friend of my brothers, a terrible accident caused by wet and leaf covered roads and street lamps without light sent him, and us, into a skid that ended up with his car wrapped around a telephone pole.

Life changed unalterably for us all. Two died, one never regained normal consciousness, and only two survived, my 19-year-old brother and me. The difference between us was he flew out of the front broken windshield sustaining only shock and a skinned elbow, whilst I was trapped in the car by both legs, one under the front seat broken at the ankle, one under the back seat, the side back window put out by my head, and a compound fracture of my right thigh in 33 places.

As words are not enough to tell all, I will go to the comparison with my present isolation and sense of paralysis. For three months I was in traction in a hospital bed, sharing the 2-person room with a succession of adults ranging in age from 19 to 87, during which time parents and friends of my brother and I visited regularly, driving the amicable Ward nurse to distraction with Hootenannies. My mother began reading me chapters from *Alice in Wonderland & Through the Looking Glass* in afternoon visits that she continued when I was home for 2 months in a cast that went up my right leg and around my hips. I had only one tutor, a delightful retired English teacher with upswept blue tinted hair who taught me how to write from my own experience. A woman from our church came and taught me how to hand sculpt with clay. She told me wonderful stories of her antics as a youth and since. My father always prayed with me at the end of each visit to the hospital.

I did sleep a lot, watched the little television someone gave me, and talked with my changing roommates learning from their very different lives and experiences.

Of course, there were no internet distractions or cell phone communications, but I kept engaged in life from my hospital bed as I slowly healed.

Isn't this what we are all asked to do, more or less, now, as we practice staying at home, or social distancing, and wearing of face covering masks? We need to make the most of the world around us as it is, now, and may be for quite some time to come.

If I could do this at 15, I must be able to do so at 71 and beyond. I also can never forget that three young people never had the opportunity to explore life as I have since my recovery, these past 56 years.

God bless those who have not made it through this Virus, as well as those who have. I thank God every day for life, for friends, for music and poetry, for plays, and worship services, and all we can see and share through the internet, the telephone, and letters, even hand-written, to stay in touch. Spring's foliage, flowers and birds carry on as always.

My past and present are intertwined.

© Chelsea Bradway

"In regard to why we decided to be in The Front Steps Project, we wanted to document this unprecedented time to share with our children as they get older. We hope that 70 years from now, our sons can tell their grandchildren how they were alive for the COVID-19 pandemic and about the role their parents played in helping people."

~ Lisa McNair ~

Boos and Yays for Quarantine!

Margie Wiggin

I wrote this poem on 4/7/2020, to encourage people to look forward, not knowing how long we would be quarantined, and to see that some good could come from this difficult time.

Margie Wiggin grew up as the oldest of four, with a creative, musical, optimistic father and a fun, funny, librarian mother. She is a single mom of two daughters and a son, ages 19-32. She has lived in Hopkinton for 27 years and tries to find the good in every situation.

Boos and Yays for Quarantine!

It started on St Patrick's Day,
no cheering with green beer...

Palm Sunday came and went,
waving palms will come next year...

Passover followed next,
Matzos online with family dear...

The Easter Bunny still arrived,
Heralding Spring without any fear...

Then May Day was in full swing,
lovely flowers and lighter gear...

By Mother's Day, there was more hope,
that no distancing we would hear...

And soon enough, we'll be free to move,
to walk, to talk, to touch with no fear...

Never again would we take for granted,
hugging, dancing, our distance disappears...

Being together, spending time,
closer than 6 feet from ear to ear

Knowing now, we are united,
knowing we should share with our peers...

Not stockpile stuff, like toilet paper,
just take what we need, that's clear...

Reaching out to stay connected,
thanking heroes, for them we cheer! ...

Appreciating the important little things,
loving, helping, sharing a tear...

Staying apart brought us together again,
our future looks bright, though I'm not a seer...

Resetting our values, making life better,
cherishing family and freedom, that's clear...

Saying boo and yay for quarantine,
we made history and we're still here!!!

Calling Bird

Steve Rapson

Steve Rapson is a solo guitarist, songwriter, and author of *The Art of the Soloperformer: A Field Guide to Stage & Podium.* www.steverapson.com

Calling Bird
© 2013

There's a calling bird
Singing in the wood
Music to my ears
He's sounding pretty good

I hear him night and day
With no one answering
Alone in the trees
Still he always sings

> Like a calling bird
> We all sing our song
> Even if no one
> Wants to sing along

> But if someone hears
> And wants to sing with you
> Where there was one song...
> Now there are two

> > Sing your song
> > Sing your song

© Christine Strickland Photography

"We decided to participate because we felt it would be nice to add diversity of family composition to the project knowing our town does not have many single-parent families. Also, I wanted to represent Nurses in my community during the pandemic."

~ The Michaud Family ~

Moonlight

Bruce Marcus

I submit the poem for the same reason the title narrator of Moonlight dances on the water.

Bruce Marcus is a storyteller, writer and performing artist who has been sharing his fresh-as-mint original stories, songs, poems and miscellany with audiences throughout New England since 1990.

Moonlight

I am moonlight.

And I beheld one night,
far from any village,
a young man out walking.
He seemed to be contemplating something,
though I know not what,
for he never said a word,
but rather stared at the ground with a scowl,
as he walked along,
far from any village.
Perhaps it was a woman who occupied his thoughts,
or perhaps his tenure on earth,
but he never said a word until,
by the pond that stood at the edge of a field,
he lay himself down to sleep
and said, to no one there,
"Goodnight."

And as he slept, I stayed close,
for he was but a man,
and far, as I've said, from any village.

When later he awoke,
he seemed confused by the stars,
which had shifted in the blackness.
He sat facing the pond,
hugging his knees tightly,

and I, finding he was watching,
danced for him on the water.
A breeze blew up and I was a bright, sinewy serpent,
reaching out toward him across that pond.
And then the breeze was quiet and I was a shiny silver dollar,
bobbing on the surface
just out of reach.

He watched me this way a while,
until finally he rose to leave,
returning, I believe,
to the place where he belonged.
And as he walked along, I believe he understood
– though for sure I know not,
for he never said another word –
understood that, even beneath a shifting sky,
he too must perform his dance,
and hope that the right eyes might see.

A Motherless Child's Odyssey to Adulthood

Barbara Aliprantis

A life-long high-energy quintessential optimist, born with a quirky sense of humor, a sunny disposition and the "gift of gab," I confronted head-on the death of my mother when I was 3-1/2 years old, with the help and support of my widowed father. A lifetime later, the proud mother of two successful grown sons, the memory of that life-altering event compelled me to compose this poem in an NYU Drama Therapy Workshop.

Barbara Aliprantis, a nationally acclaimed Bilingual (English/ASL) Greek-American Storyteller, is the recipient of the 2018 Northeast Storytelling Brother Blue and Ruth Hill Award, a National Storytelling Network Oracle Award, and she was honored at New York City Hall "… for her commitment to sharing multi-cultural folklore and immigrants' experiences for both hearing and non-hearing audiences around the country."

A Motherless Child's Odyssey to Adulthood

"It is the image in the mind that links us to our lost treasures, but it is the loss that gathers the flowers, weaves the garland." – Colette, My Mother's House

"What say you?"
The world said,
as it dropped the small child on her head...

"What's your problem?
You can sit and cry
or get up on your feet
it matters not to the world, you see!"

"Oh yeah" said the girl child, with a determined grin,
"Go ahead, drop me again. It matters not what you do to me,
cause I'll survive, no matter what, wait and see…"

The little girl stood up.
Dusted off her duff,
hell bent to show the world her stuff!

She sang, she danced, stood on her head,
she listened. She talked.
She did what they said.

Then, at the age of eighteen,
I picked up a brush
and painted the injustices my eyes had seen.

I tried through my paintings to make THEM see.
What was wrong with our world, was killing me.
What else could I do?
I forged ahead as a bleeding-heart liberal.

Now this poet could continue this rambling rhyme
but alas, she's afraid she'll run out of time
so, she'll wrap it up by addressing the question at hand:

Should she continue to bleed from her heart and soul...
Continue doing what she is told?
Or should she allow herself to feel what she feels,
doing just what she believes is right?

Sharing herself, with herself, and worrying not
if the world can't see what she sees,
letting go of that constant voice in her head
which resonates so loud that it is hard for her to understand
that her skull has healed from the original blow!

So, get on with your life dear Barbara of mine
the invisible issue can now be put to rest
cause you're quite a "human doing genius" and a wonderful self.

If we listen to the stories our children tell.
Listen to the stories we tell ourselves.
Perhaps we will understand the plight of people less fortunate than you or
me.

Poem for Mary Oliver

Tom Sloan

When the pandemic hit and we were all in lockdown, I decided to post a photo a day for 30 straight days on my social media accounts. These were landscape photos that I'd captured in Hopkinton and I called the series Hopkinton Light. One of the photos inspired me to write this poem of hope, faith, and gratitude – themes that come through in Mary Oliver's works. Her poem "The House of Light" is my favorite poem and it ties so well into photography – where it's all about the light.

Tom Sloan has lived in Hopkinton, MA for the past 12 years and enjoys capturing photos of the beautiful scenes around town. He is an IT professional but enjoys landscape and portrait photography.

Poem for Mary Oliver

Her words are a house of light,
carrying with them the hope,
the faith,
the promise of new days to come.

In this tranquil dawn,
no ripples
on the still scene
before me,
reflections unfold.

Patient sun rising,
shafts of light gleaming,
a dazzling dance of color
never to be repeated,
a visual array of promises –
promises of hope.

Standing knee deep in the water,
I see the island in reflection.
Its silhouette rising up,
breathing new life,

another gift intended
for me to capture.

What will be,
slowly unfolds.

The mist breaking
and rising up,
then gone,
as the sun warms the water
that surrounds me.

In these moments,
I realize that we are all observers,
caretakers,
on temporary watch.
Witnesses to His artistry.

The canvas is always prepared.
We just need to show up
and we will be treated
to His masterpiece –
His house of light.

We must bear witness.
So, I click the shutter,
to let the light in.

For, as she said,
the light is everything.

Are We Masking Our Emotions?

Elizabeth Ricketson

The pandemic in a most dramatic way altered our lives in a significant fashion. The gift during this curious period of time has been the perceivable soulful thoughtfulness felt by many. The intangibles of human existence, love, family and small kindnesses gave meaning once again to life during COVID-19.

A graduate of Providence College with a BA in English, Elizabeth Ricketson has always had a love of literature and the fine arts. In the 1990s, she studied figure drawing at the Rhode Island School of Design spending years dedicated to understanding human form, movement and anatomy. Freelance writer, published essayist and author of a blog titled "It's Complicated." Website: https://elizabeth-ricketson.com. Elizabeth's essays focus on life experiences and life in Vermont. Elizabeth Ricketson works and resides in South Pomfret, VT with her husband Jon and dog Cub.

Are We Masking Our Emotions?

A big week as I planned my first social distancing meeting with a friend yesterday. She suggested three meeting places while allowing me to decide on what would feel the most comfortable during this time of social distancing. I selected the most open space area with the probability of the least likely amount of people. I reminded myself that this is Vermont and not downtown Boston. The extra added bonus being that the location was just a few miles from my home. Perfect day for a bike ride. The sun was strong, a cooling breeze and a simple ride.

Starting down the road the immediate feel of freedom washed over me. A childlike freedom. The most genuine type of freedom. I was remembering summer bike rides to reach any and all destinations. Friends' houses, sandlot ball games, Mr. Baker's Corner Store. Just near the store wooden counter with Mr. Baker at the register sat a deep white freezer with a sliding heavy scratched glass cover. Each scratch giving evidence of the many children and the many sales before me. Children like me that stood high on their toes reaching deep down into the freezer with their hands, arms and a small portion of their upper body. Reaching for fudgsicles, popsicles or possibly a hoodsie. The freezer had thick walls of ice making the ice cream impossibly hard to eat without the warmth of the outdoors to aid the thaw. Childhood memories ... great memories.

My ride was straight forward and relaxed. Noticing the few cars that passed me in both directions possessed out of state license plates which "normally" would not stand out as Memorial Day is upon us. Second homes become occupied once again as last visited might have been ski season. Tourism would normally be upon us and welcome as it is an important part of our Vermont economy. But notable it is now. Are they self-quarantining?

My only other bike traveler was a young boy of 8, 9 or maybe 10 years of age. He was wearing a red sports jersey and more specifically a Boston Red Sox jersey. I imagined what a beautiful day it would have been to be at Fenway Park to watch a game. The crisp white uniforms as the players take the manicured field is one of my very favorite moments at the start of a baseball game. I could imagine it, hear the sounds of fans settling in and the vendors shouting peanuts, popcorn, hot dogs! Ice Cold Beer! Summer. Summer sounds. Summer life. I noticed the young boy had pulled to the side of the road and as I passed by, I glanced over to see if he was ok and he was. He was attending to his mask. More accurately he was putting his mask on. One can't help but wonder if he was heading home and meeting a parent's mask requirement? Had he left the house with the mask on, rode just enough distance to be out of site and removed it? I understand as it is hard to exercise with a mask on. This will be an issue as kids will be kids. I remember making my own fashion adjustments on the school bus going to school once out of my parent's view ... my mother's all-knowing view. The difference being now there are much more dramatic consequences. How do we manage this? How to live childlike yet safely ...

The afternoon had all the lovely elements of a lazy unofficial summer day albeit a Thursday. Hours, days, weeks and now months have lost their structure and meaning. One travels light on a bike as my bike saddle had just enough room for the emergency tire repair items in case of a dreaded flat. No bike shirt today as I was visiting with a friend. No phone, no watch ... no recognition of time with the exception of our meeting time. I arrived. Found a place to lean my bike, a picnic table to sit at while I waited for my friend to arrive. Landscapers were busy grooming the vast lawn. A young family working on their CSA (Community Supported Agriculture). A father and son laughing and talking as they navigated the wheel barrel for more dirt. Both wearing masks, the son's a youthful pattern while dad sported a solid blue. Their lively conversation and laughter were as relaxed and playful as in usual times and maskless times. I guess we are managing. We are adapting.

I sat quietly while I waited five or maybe it was ten minutes as I had no device to confirm how long. The sun brightly shining down on my face felt warm and reassuring. It dawned on me that we will soon have a new definition for tan lines!!!! Will our masks create an image similar to a clown's white and extended mouth? Instagram posts will be quite entertaining as we continue to live in a not so entertaining time. We are certainly trying to make the best of our circumstance as we move forward with some calculated risks.

Happy to see my friend and we settled into a socially distanced chat. She sported a very cute mask. Maybe orange is the new black but are masks our new fashion statement? We sat many feet apart but no less engaged in conversation. Chatting with a new friend who has quickly become a dear friend. We had time to learn about each other. Time for questions. Time for more thoughtful and expansive answers. Very nice indeed. A meaningful conversation with a stunning Vermont background. Hours passed without notice. A welcome new friendship. Moving is hard. Being relatively new in an area is even harder. Grateful.

The ride home was a little slower as I took the time to enjoy the beauty around me. I passed just a few houses as is common in Vermont, but people were sitting in their yards waving and saying hello as I rode by...

A different kind of warmth brought me all the way home...

Exposure of Sheltering

James Ph. Kotsybar

One of the earliest philosophers remarked, "I am not so much upset by events as by how I perceive them." I believe that, despite loss and all the world's ills, hope and even joy can be found again.

James Ph. Kotsybar is the first poet published to another planet. Repeatedly chosen for NASA's special recognition, his poetry orbits Mars aboard NASA's MAVEN spacecraft, appears in the Hubble Space Telescope's mission log and was awarded and featured at NASA's Centaur Art Challenge at IngenuityFest, Ohio. Invited by the president of the European Academy of Sciences Arts and Letters in 2018, he performed his poetry before an international audience of scientists and Troubadours (Europe's oldest poetic institution) in their founding city of Toulouse, France, at the EuroScience Open Forum, earning a standing return invitation.

Exposure of Sheltering

The jigsaw puzzle has been completed
and has been on the counter for a week.
The days are longer; rains have receded,
but COVID-19 in our state's not reached its peak.

We work on cars, or garden, just to see
the random neighbor, masked, out for a jog
or checking on postal delivery
or, distanced by leash length, walking the dog.

We're gladdened to wave to one another
and know real human contact still exists,
though none may see the "smile on your brother,"
through masks, outside shelters, culture persists.

We'll return to healthy, wealthy and wise.
It won't be through division (no surprise).

A Long Hard Climb

Michael Santoro

I submitted my lyrics for "A Long Hard Climb" to the Words of Hope Project because I liked the idea of using climbing a mountain as a metaphor for overcoming adversity in life, and it seemed to fit the times that we are in with the COVID-19 pandemic.

Michael Santoro has always had a connection to music as far back as he can remember. Early in life, he learned to play an instrument and then went on to play in bands. Later in his life, after a lull of not being involved with music, he began trying to write songs and perform his original material. He became enthralled with the process and the struggle of creating a story within the constraints of a metered melody.

A Long Hard Climb

I can see a mountaintop
Rising in the distance
And I take it as a sign
And I'm gonna take the steps
To continue my existence
I'm ready for a long, long hard climb

I'm feeling just a little pain
As I'm traveling the distance
But I can see the sunlight through the pines
Then I reach down deep inside
And overcome my resistance
I'm ready for a long, long hard climb

Now I'm drinking from a mountain stream
I'm listening to the birds sing
I stop and rest
I look down into the valley
I can see the green, green grass
It gives me a strength that will last

Now I'm standing on the mountaintop
A reward to my persistence
I reach up and touch the deep blue sky
Then I see another mountaintop
It's standing in the distance
And I'm ready for a long, long hard climb
I'm ready for a long, long hard climb
I'm ready for a long hard climb

Tongues in Trees

Joan Alice Wood Kimball

In "Tongues in Trees," the narrator finds solace and peace in meditation, and hope in nature's energy.

Joan Alice Wood Kimball runs poetry workshops in Wayland & Concord, Mass. For five years she performed humorous verse with the troupe, *X. J. Kennedy & the Light Brigade*. She has appeared in many journals and anthologies. She published two illustrated chapbooks, edited a third, and her collection, *Early Light*, came out in 2019 from Kelsay Books. Her limerick, "Cold October," is inscribed on granite in Edmands Park, Newton, MA.

Tongues in Trees

Exiled to the Forest of Arden, the Duke finds "tongues in trees, books in the running brooks, sermons in stones, and good in everything." --- Shakespeare, *As You Like It*. II, 1, 12.

On the path to the pond, the breeze
makes pines and maples shiver.
Listen to the trees that shake their
natal finger tips in spring.

Their lined-up trunks are temple columns,
bracing the forest ceiling on their heads.
Listen to a pecking bird drumming on bark,
while a vireo darts from branch to branch.

Sitting on this cabin's wooden porch, palms together,
I'll honor the birds who open their throats to chatter:
the dove's coo, followed by the cardinal's "tee-you"
and a robin's squeaky scold, "Heed my whistle: wuck! wuck!"

I see the pond in sunlight beyond the trees:
an outdoor ballroom with a ceiling of blue.
The pond disburses water lilies—balls of white,
strewn across a five-acre bowling green.

A casual exile from the world, I
watch summer's oven breeze court the trees,
the skittish butterflies, the prying birds.

I count my breath as the woods stitch closed their ceiling
sealing out the sky. All disappear and there remain
cupped hands, the whispering canopy and raw terrain.

Written on the porch of the Meditation Hut at Old Frog Pond Farm.

Transplant

Carla Schwartz

My poem, Transplant, speaks to a personal challenge of living through quarantine and owning a home that the speaker no longer wants. The poem finds the speaker uprooting herself, while at the same time, the speaker finds hope and solace in the uprooting of her favorite garden plants to bring with her, to transplant to her new home, along with herself.

Filmmaker and photographer Carla Schwartz's poems have been widely published and anthologized, including in *The Practicing Poet* (Diane Lockward, Ed), and in her second collection, *Intimacy with the Wind*, (Finishing Line, 2017). Her CB99videos YouTube channel has 2,000,000+ views. Learn more at carlapoet.com, wakewiththesun.blogspot.com, or find her on YouTube, Twitter, or Instagram @cb99videos.

Transplant

Home, after many days' work,
many days' pleasure
from my new life,
my quarantine life
with my lover
to my empty house,
which isn't as empty
as it needs to be,
because, now that I've moved out
prodded by the pandemic
I plan to sell,
but I worry how
I can possibly purge
my household,
when everything's closed
and I think about all I will miss —
the raspberry patches
I trim back spring and fall,
the boom or bust peach tree
whose blooms I'm timid to cull,
the butterfly plants I spread the seeds of

in my side yard
in defiance of my neighbor
who complains when the flowers dry up,
even the lemon yellow daffodils
I planted years ago —

so I plan the uprooting —
the raspberry shoots,
rhubarb, tulips,
stealing from myself
in stealth,
because I'm practicing
invisibility,
because even in this pandemic,
my neighbor makes
inordinate demands,
so now I bend over my shovel,
and from behind the cloak
of my overgrown rhododendron,
I begin to dig.

Bee Quest

Michele Boule

I wrote the first draft of this poem approximately six months after my late (unofficial) husband died from ALS. It had been quite the journey traveling his illness with him, a strange mix of shock and grief, of helplessness and yet a heightened appreciation for the beauty still prominent in life, for the wonderfulness that pain cannot tarnish, the light that forces its way into daily experience. Acceptance of the inevitable can be a strange friend, a strange experience and yet very freeing in a way.

Michele Boule has lived in the Acton area for over 20 years and has participated in various open mics, reading and performing poetry and playing some piano as well. She has a background in Fine Arts but has held various positions in diversified day-jobs including banking, television production and biotech (pays those bills). She has been divorced and widowed (not the same people) and she has a wonderful son, now 29, living in the Bay area in CA.

Bee Quest

that kind of Winter
your matted pelt pulls so tight around your hungry bones
and you dream of trees leafy with green
and you sniff for bees buzzing slow with sleep
that kind of Spring brings the arduous climb
to higher branches for the view of endless sky
And maybe bees
warm winds ruffle your sweaty fur
shedding now in great mildewed clumps
as you creep upward, branch by branch
hoping for bees alive with honey
while clear clean clouds beg for a higher climb
then the top is here, a diamond-sharp blue
then your losing grip, your ravaged paws so hungry
and the fall, fall, free-fall spiraling downward
like falling in love
plummeting such a long way down
but stops
abruptly

before the disaster of hard ground
and prompts a wild urge to fly
to leave damp dirt once again
you sprout feathers from the middle of your back
making a tiny flap
and incandescent wings grow like a bee's
tiny and translucent yet mighty with the power of wind
enough to keep you flying,
soaring over trees near clouds, smelling honey
your discarded fur scattering the ground below

the small things:
wings and honey, clouds and leaves, blue sky and gossamer wings
We wake from darkness, and search for radiance
the smell of honey
the sound of leaves
and
oh .... those beautiful bees

Morning Contemplations

Linda Havel

I enjoy moments in the backyard, in the company of dragonflies and chipmunks, imagining all, friends, family and children, before pandemic time here, all encourage me to write another poem.

As Linda Havel began to write and tell stories, some evolved into poetry, opening possibilities for her to awaken and participate... to use experiences from life, as a daughter, sister, spouse, mother, and grandmother. In 1987, she received a B.S. in Life Cycle Development with Concentration in Aging/Family/ Psychology from Lesley University, Cambridge, MA.

Morning Contemplations

Here, chipmunk dashes into a dark tunnel,
dragonflies pry into daylily buds' secrets.

In this backyard where everything flies,
skitters past me, I'm in shade of umbrella

above me. Below me, I want to trust uneven
redwood boards, each one nailed to wooden

beams, with years of disintegration underneath
our old deck. Happily, I'm in the wake of songbirds

and sunshine, and cannot imagine any signs of ruin
either inside chipmunk's underground world, or

in this surround of wonder. Along with morning coffee,
and feeling reminders of change, other times, children,

I can imagine stories, not about what is missed, I'll tell
about our expanded family, our new friends gathering.

© Lynne Damianos

"We participated in this project because it was a great medium to bring people together virtually when they could not see each other in person. It made us feel like we were part of our community and the greater community beyond.

We also wanted photographic evidence of 2020 that we can look back on in the future and say 'That was the time when...' "

~ **The Pilkington-Sperry Family** ~

The Bird

Ellen S. Bettmann Piontek

The Bird was inspired by my first cousin, Joen Bettmann who passed away in May. She was a lover of life, children, family, cooking, and silliness. She inspired others, through her personal relationships and her Montessori International Training Schools, where she often became a lifetime mentor to her adult international students, and her biggest goal was to spread world peace. She also brought Montessori to Israel and parts of Africa.

Ellen S. Bettmann Piontek is a bird lover and animal lover who playfully envisions what could be and professionally has been in the human services profession and mental health field for over 35 years. This story is written with the hope that world peace will become a reality and that in the meantime, a loving bird is watching over all of us. It is dedicated to Ellen's Grandchildren.

The Bird

A fleeting moment.

In flight, to places unknown even to most students of life. Many senses of direction. Absorbing life's gifts of love and beauty, by spreading her wings. Watch me fly! Watch me soar! Follow me and then follow your own heart and trust the beat as you glide, and dance and we'll get where we're meant to go. Even if it wasn't part of the plan. Now it is. Or maybe it was all along. The universe does not reveal all of her secrets. Certainly not all at once.

Peace!

With so many unknowns and drops of self-doubt on a rainy day. Just listen. Listen. The answers will come. And the answers give way to more questions. She persists in a direction, adjusting wings with both flexibility and determination, and with steady and consistent encouragement, to those who learn by following. And then experimenting. And learning to love the journey, not only the destination.

Peace!

The bird couples and creates a nest both inviting and intriguing. Others flock there and begin to mature and embrace their own strengths. The food on the menu every single day is compassion. Compassion being the sustenance which the bird happily wiggles down her throat to feel that squishy warm feeling. Squiggle, squiggle. Yum.

Flight of thought. A family tradition.

Peace!

And so.
The bird spreads her long and graceful wings, gliding over the ocean and then with a clear view and a glimpse of the future she sails over the beach. Safe travels. Home. Again, and again. Home.

Peace!

With her own brand of grace, she brakes a bit, onto the sand, inhaling warmth, and oh the salt and the sounds near and far… and with toes spread and running, she leaves bird-style footprints forever and a day, and the children run fast as they can or at times hopping and skipping behind, and try to fill those shapes with their teeny feet... while giggling and squealing with delight.

Peace!

Magical moments are never forgotten. Imprinted on the small children's being, as a map and certain path. Perhaps it will lead others to tip toe on the rainbow. Or a flying elephant might land on the kitchen window- sill, peer in and wonder what's for dinner. What do I crave? What do I long for? What more is there to explore? How can I see it all without a bird's-eye view?

Inhale. Exhale.

Peace!

A calling and a response… With all of the senses awakened by flowers, nourishing foods, the sun and blue sky on this new day. The sound is unmistakable. It's remarkable. It's achievable. The sound is …

Peace!
Peace!
Peace!

A Song for Those Who Cannot Sing

Paul Szlosek

I feel that my poem "A Song For Those Who Cannot Sing", even though it is a bit silly, it also truly sends a message of hope, that even though we may feel frustrated and perhaps incapable of singing, we all can still share and express the music within our hearts with others by writing poetry...

Paul Szlosek is a poet living in Worcester, MA and also a co-founder and co-host of The Poetorium at Starlite Reading Series & Open Mic Series in Southbridge. A past recipient of the Jacob Knight Award for Poetry, he just recently placed third in the 2020 Frank O'Tara Poetry Prize.

A Song for Those Who Cannot Sing

This is a song for those who cannot sing
a song for those who cannot bring
the music in their hearts into the world
without someone screaming,
"Pipe down and cut out that caterwauling!"

This is a song for the sixth grade boy
who is told by his singing coach
he has a range of just two notes -
both of them off-key.

This is a song for those whom carrying a tune
is a lot like carrying some foul-smelling
liquid in a sieve -
something's flowing but it sure ain't no melody!

This is a song for those who can only
let their voices ring out
under the cover of the auditory camouflage
of running water or heavy machinery
unless they be mistaken for the family pet
being sucked down the garbage disposal.

This is a song, a simple reminder
that in singing, like in most endeavours
those who can -
flaunt it in our faces.
Those who cannot -
whine and write poetry!

What is Hope?

Arhan Shrivastava

submitting this poem to bring hope to people and give them a reason to smile.

an Shrivastava is a 7th grade student at Hopkinton Middle School and he
es to read and play soccer.

What is Hope?

Hope is what holds us to reality
Yet sometimes pulls us away
It can help you through times of despair
And it is everywhere even in the air
Without hope we would be lost
Not knowing what to do next
All our dreams would fade away
Just like the great T-Rex
With every single turn we make
Our great hope is there
Sometimes it just makes me think
How can we make it fair?

"This project was so much fun! Due to many unforeseen circumstances, we were very excited to have the opportunity to participate and spread the joy. These pictures sure helped to brighten our day and our minds. Thank you!

~ The Nation Family ~

Heroes of the World

Prisha Shrivastava

I am submitting this poem to inspire hope in people. Be someone's hero.

Prisha Shrivastava is a 9th grade student at Hopkinton High School. She likes to draw, bake, play piano and soccer. She likes to read a lot too.

Heroes of the World

The world is a crazy place
It can be many things, whether they are good or bad
But it can only be as crazy as the people on it
And it can also be as peaceful as the people on it
Because whatever the world throws at us
We were made to overcome that
We don't have the help of superheroes with supernatural abilities
But we have heroes of our own who are pulling us through
The best thing about the effort for COVID-19 relief
Is that you don't have to be a doctor to be a hero
Facetiming a friend
Playing a song for someone
Making masks for those who need them
Anything you do to help cheer up others
Makes you a hero
So even though these are dark times
A team effort will soon bring brighter days

That Silver Lining

Pooja Shrivastava

I am submitting this poem as this pandemic has changed lives, taken lives and has not left anyone untouched. I hope to fill some hope in any heart that needs it.

Pooja Shrivastava works in Application Development at CVS Health. She is a mother of two and loves to spend time with her family, read, write and help people.

That Silver Lining

Baby rays of sunshine
say hello to my bedroom window.
Before my eyes can open
my loving husband, I know,
is already out exercising,
Running and sweltering.
Making the world seem
embarrassingly loafing.
He motivates friends and family,
neighbors and community.
With his un-swayed discipline
Of exercise and nutrition.

My daughter's hard at work
turning kitchen island into an oasis
Not of greens but chocolate,
Carrot and red velvet cookies
Pizza, pasta, lasagna, now
samosas too are a breeze.
With intent and spirited eyes,
She takes on the challenge.
To see her dad savor cookies
free of sugar and gluten.

My son's smile holding his guitar in style
brightens up the day
He creates beautiful music,

And all the noise in the house.
That keeps the home alive,
Tempting neighbors to browse.
Every morning without fail,
he makes his bed so neat,
My heart's as proud as can be
and just skips a beat.

Dinnertime calls for teamwork,
my team's hard-working.
Cooking, decorating, serving, cleaning
and even entertaining.
Meals don't have to be a chore
or quick fix anymore.
With creative chefs' appetizers,
main courses, desserts galore.

The pandemic rendered my evenings
to be just family time.
Earlier what we couldn't afford
is now dozen a dime.
Walking, talking, biking, running,
playing in yard and driveway
Hop scotch, pittoo, spud, soccer, four-square,
throw & catch, while a new game is on its way.

With my husband and kids,
at home around the clock,
We feel so much like
birds of a flock.
But seeing the pandemic causing
havoc in the air,
I pray and try to keep my
family safe inside here.

For my world outside beyond,
Not sure what those
Golden words would be,
That can bring hope to
A grieving heart you see.
Left mourning by a soul that departed,
Without a hug or goodbye.
Don't let go of that silver lining

That will present itself,
only if you try.

Think how much your life
That person influenced.
Think what hopes and dreams
That person would transcend.
Give back to the world not just your share,
but also the one crossed.
And live not just your life,
But also the one lost.

On New Normals

Daniel Levinson

I've been keeping a care journal for friends and relatives, ever since my wife had a significant cerebral hemorrhage at the end of 2017. The friend I have known longest in my 71 years suggested I submit a recent entry for this collection. Unfortunately, our personal tragedy intersected with an international disaster, and writing through both great calamities has helped keep me from dissolving in anxiety and fear. It makes sense that many people would also need to write themselves through the COVID-19 crisis.

Daniel Levinson taught English and History, Journalism and Philosophy for over 40 years at Thayer Academy in Braintree, MA. He has written in a variety of forms over those years, staying true to the little boy who fondly remembers playing with an ink block printer set.

On New Normals

"People wish to be settled… (but) only as far as they are unsettled is there any hope for them." ---Emerson

Billions of people around the world are working through their own thinking and adjusting to the idea of a "New Normal" (NN) now. Or trying to. There are so many unforeseen, unforeseeable, aspects of this NN that the situation is profoundly unsettling.

I have been living day after day with a big NN for over two years now (since my wife Cindy's serious cerebral hemorrhage), and have seen some of Emerson's upside: needing to be and do better to meet the challenge of the changes. There are obvious and less obvious downsides to being so unsettled too.

The collisions and oscillations of grief and gratitude, hope and fear after life has changed forever in a dire way can be disorienting. And even when all that seems to become familiar, the destabilizing reverberations work beneath the surface. There's also a difference, I've discovered, between immediate crisis mode and living with new emotional weight long term. At any given moment life seems the same, but living in extreme emotional circumstances left me — before the new pandemic stressors — noticing that if a little more weight is piled on the day, I feel very quickly that it's close to being too much. It may not be, but it feels so.

Every day brings its share of moments where I look at Cindy with wonder, marveling at how much she is at that moment. And every day brings its moments of seeing devastating, irretrievable loss that I try not to think about because she is here and I am here and that means we both have to do the best we can with that mix. I try, too, not to think about how much her quality of life totally depends on me. So I try not to think (too often) about the real weight of things to do what I need to do. I try to keep in mind that I don't want to sink too unconsciously into the habits of normality, as much as I appreciate them, to keep deeper needs in mind. I have to constantly reset to that star to keep anxieties from overwhelming me. But I've always been a fretter.

And Cindy? She reacts with moments of despair only occasionally. Luckily — at least for that aspect of our NN — It fits her condition: she's at her sharpest, her most confused, her most energetic, her most listless, her happiest, saddest, most skillful, most helpless — in pretty unpredictable ways, moment to moment, day to day. That makes some aspects of our life easier, some harder. With the possibility of new satisfactions to replace some of what's lost. NN.

Taking It In

Hibiscus Rose

Living in the present moment has assisted me the most in living through the pandemic and that is why I submitted the poem, "Taking It In."

Hibiscus Rose is a Hopkinton resident. She has connected with many other poets since moving to Hopkinton sixteen years ago. She is blessed with five wonderful daughters and twelve beautiful grandchildren and four lovely step-grandchildren.

Taking It In

Sitting quietly,
attentive to life,
watching,
listening,
taking it in.

The sky e'er
so blue,
the trees
gentle rustling,

moment to moment,
life in the present,
watching,
listening,
taking it in.

"We chose to commemorate our daughter Mikayla's senior year. Mikayla is an introvert, so this senior year was amazing! She had prayed for 'snow days' but was just as happy with 'Corona days!'"

~ The Cappetta Family ~

The Answer Is...

Alan O'Hare

For countless eons now, we humans have been blessed with so many gifts that continually awaken each of us, and at the same time we have been blessed with many more questions that create an endless river of questions to discover anew the daily art of being alive. So, with a deep and equal sense of gratitude for the answers, but also the questions that open us to many more opportunities and creations, I am honored to celebrate equally a poem/song entitled: The Answer Is ...

Alan O' Hare is a seanchie, a storyteller from the ancient Celtic tradition, who has created over twenty plays and more than one hundred original stories, as well as awakened the tales of countless people and communities regionally, nationally and internationally. He is also the Director of Life Story Theatre and a retired adjunct faculty member at Lesley University Graduate Expressive Arts Therapy Program, where he taught and learned Storytelling and Healing with and from his students.

The Answer Is...

In all the world where we wander
from day to day, morn to night

how we going to pray
how we going to light

how we going to share
how we going to fight

how we going to work
how we going to play

how we going to love
how we going to dream

then wake up crying
just ready to scream

the answer is simple
the same time it's hard

you reach out all over
but it's in your backyard

the answer's not money
nor another new toy

the answer is simple
the answer is joy

the answer is faith
the answer is joy

the answer is hope
the answer is joy

the answer is love
the answer is joy

the answer is song
the answer is joy

the answer is dance
the answer is joy

there's no other answer
the answer is joy

do you hear what I'm saying
in all the world's places

that covers all cultures
that embraces all races

it's not more possessions
it's not some more plans

it's not another venture
into more far away lands

the answer is holy

the answer is joy

the answer is here
the answer is joy

the answer is now
the answer is joy

in a sister, in a brother
the answer is joy

reach out to each other
the answer is joy

reach high, reach low
same answer is joy

reach up far above
the answer is joy

wherever you go
the answer is joy

at every new birth
the answer is joy

at the end of a life
the answer is joy

alleluja alleluja
the answer is joy

alleluja alleluja
the answer is joy

thank you to all
the answer is joy

thank you holy one
the answer is joy

the answer is joy
the answer is joy

the answer is joy
the answer is joy

The End...and
The Beginning

Healing with the Stone

Dot Walsh

This poem honors the many people throughout the world who suffered the loss of loved ones during the COVID-19 pandemic, as well as hospital personnel, workers who provided transportation, food, necessary medication and everyone who offered their empathy through actions and faith. I submitted this poem because hope is eternal and needed for grounding so that we can continue on finding strength to create new paths for healing. My poem was inspired by "Stonewalk" which was created to allow civilians who died as a result of war throughout the world to be honored and remembered. A one-ton stone was carved and placed on a caisson and pulled along streets from city to city. It began in the United States in 1999 and continued on in future years to Ireland, England, Boston to New York after 9/11, Japan and Korea. A Stonewalk from Boston to New York is planned for 2021 or whenever it is safe to do so. Recently the caisson was renovated in preparation as the stone will be arriving soon.

Dot Walsh is a Peace Chaplain from the world-renowned Peace Abbey of Sherborn, MA. founded and directed by Lewis Randa. This Center honors Courage of Conscience leaders, organizations, and peacebuilders from around the world. Included in the recipients are Archbishop Desmond Tutu, Nelson Mandela and Mother Teresa. Dot has a long history in Human Service Management, which includes Staff Training and Supervision, Pastoral Counseling, and Spiritual Direction. Most recently she has been the Cable Television Creator and Host for "Oneness and Wellness" – discussing topics and techniques of finding emotional balance and well-being in today's busy and turbulent world. She is author of *Finding Light in the Darkness: Stories from Prison that Bear Witness to Hope, Faith and Love Despite Man's Inhumanity to Man* - True stories based on 20 years working as part of a chaplaincy team in the Criminal Justice System.

Healing with the Stone

Feeling gratitude for the blessing of the day
Opening my heart aware of the many who suffer
Sending each one a prayer clothed in love
As I place my hand on the stone

Remembering family, friends and the unknown
Thanking so many who helped in so many ways

Telling our stories
Yearning to live differently
Trying to keep ourselves and others safe
Helping to pull the stone as our gift

A Gathering of Buddhas

Ji Hyang Padma

This poem commemorates a day on which our Buddhist sanghas (communities) took our most precious treasures – our Buddhas – to celebrate with all the other communities. There are a couple of thousand years of divergent culture and experiences across our traditions, in some cases: different languages, different sacred texts, different practice traditions. However, this coming together represented a faith that we could find a deeper illumination through that unity in our diversity – which is what I wish for our country at this time.

Ji Hyang Padma, Ph.D. is the Director of the Comparative Religion Program at California Institute for Human Science. She has taught Zen for twenty-five years at Wellesley College and many other institutions, currently in service of Open Gate Zen Collective. Her first book, *Living the Season: Zen Practices for Transformative Times*, was released in 2013; her second book, *Field of Blessings*, on traditional Buddhist healing practices is soon to be released.

A Gathering of Buddhas

Twenty-five years ago. Central Square, Cambridge.

Buddhists went seeking their relatives—
Sanghas of
Zen. Vipassana. Vajrayana.
Theravadan. Mahayana.
Chinese. Vietnamese. Tibetan. Korean.
Shared meals. Reunited in coalition,
and then in celebration—
celebrating the shared Path,
and its singular gifts
Vietnamese mango,
Korean pear.

Four Buddhas
one for each direction
for the corners of the earth.
Tibetan, Korean, Thai, Chinese
seated facing in

And we
various peoples
forming a circle around them
also seated.

The church
still
sheltering us
Its worn oak floors and luminous variegated glass
a prayer.

this memory of stained glass and incense
we offer
to the Buddhas
of the four directions

My Plea

Richard Leone

I submitted this poem because it was important to express my thoughts when the pandemic struck. I needed to put into words how I felt and what I hoped for the future.

It wasn't until Richard Leone was fifty that he turned to writing. As a semi-retired accountant, he wanted to use the more creative part of his brain. So now he writes poems, short stories and an occasional one-act play.

My Plea

With my saddened heart
I make this plea
That we can live
More healthily

With my wounded soul
I make this plea
To make the world
Anxious free

With my worried mind
I make this plea
That in days ahead
We breathe easily

© Christine Strickland Photography

"Not only did The Front Steps Project support our local charity, Project Just Because, it also captured a moment in time for our family that will go down in history. Our family consisted of two essential workers, an online college student and a work-from-home parent who has respiratory issues, the combination of all in one household has led us all to experience COVID-19 from different perspectives."

~ The Hayes Family ~

Your Work is a Piece of Art

Sonia Ishaq Glace

As part of our family tradition, at every birthday, we plan a RAOK (Random Act Of Kindness) to make it more meaningful. This year, on our youngest's 13th birthday, we chose to honor frontline and essential workers with a poem and a canvas. A family project to share our 'Thanks' with our heroes who courageously embraced danger to keep us safe during COVID-19 pandemic.

Sonia Ishaq Glace is a proud mother of two teenagers. With her husband and sons, she moved to Hopkinton in 2015 and is eager to connect with poets in the community to share thoughts around the importance of Empathy.

Your Work is a Piece of Art

You are our essential workers, nurses, doctors, firefighters or police officers
You are our neighbors or our friends and colleagues' sons and daughters

Your dedication during COVID-19 is inspiring, heroic and exemplary
You didn't delay or wait a second to support your community

Without the so needed test kits and PPE equipment
You never walked away from your commitment

You upped the ante and embraced danger
To beat this virus' outrageous demeanor

You are for many their hope, their heroes, their saviors
Time will remember your losses, sacrifices and favors

Keep up the good work and the fighting spirit
The days are not far when COVID-19 will exit

Play the music, chant and cheer
When your patients leave your site with joy or a tear

You are Victory, a Legend and undoubtably
For discharged patients you are making History

For the scientists and all caring souls, your work is a piece of Art
2020 made each of You our sweetheart

With immense gratitude and humility
We thank You a million for your genuine empathy

Cheers!

The Function of Faith in a Pandemic

Lisa Breger

As a cancer survivor, I know how hard it can be to stay calm and have faith up against dismal odds. When the pandemic hit, I found myself tested again, this time on a global scale. The fear is palpable, but our collective spirit is resilient, which, in itself, brings glimmers of hope.

Lisa Breger is a former Professor of English, currently working on an essay collection and book of pandemic poetry.

The Function of Faith in a Pandemic

Faith doesn't mean everything goes your way like a big score at the craps table. It doesn't mean the drowning man is saved or the sickness doesn't cripple. For many, faith is nothing more than wishful or foolish thinking, a dead end as far as pandemics are concerned. They say it's science, pure and simple, that gives hope.

Now that I'm older and have had my share of losses at the craps table of life, afflictions that left me less than myself— I see faith persisting, hanging around like a benevolent twin. Or, more precisely, the hand I hold in a time of fear. A little faith and I don't scare myself to death.
But what is it that I reach for, what exactly is faith? It's not the belief that everything is fine and will work out. It's when things don't work out, the diagnosis is worse than expected, the pandemic is worldwide, and financial ruin is insurmountable, what else is there but faith?
It's natural to want to shout, "why faith hasn't saved us, kept us from the plague. Why did God, supposed maker of all things, let this happen?"

Life happens. When challenged, I can dip my spoon in the clear well, the still waters, and know faith. I can practice all that brings me closer to this knowing: daily prayer and meditation, poetry, exercise, nature walks, bird watching, gardening. Along the way, sometimes in my darkest hour, there is the unexplainable. Perhaps a stranger comes along and tells a story, maybe bestows a kindness, and for a moment all signs illuminate the way and the darkness is no longer blindness.

I think of Nik Wallenda who performs amazing high-wire feats. He comes from a long line of acrobats, some of whom lost their lives during stunts gone wrong. Still the Flying Wallendas, as they call themselves, continue their tradition of performing aerial acts. I watched on TV as Nik Wallenda crossed Nicaragua's Masaya Volcano with the fiery crater beneath him, volcanic gases and gusts of wind and smoke swirling all around him. What struck me was how Nik thanked God or Jesus for almost every death-defying step he took. Sometimes the wind gusts were so strong he stood still and sang hymns or recited scripture as he tried to hold his balance on the swaying wire, thanking Jesus.

I feel like Nik Wallenda often as I go through my equivalents of the high-wire act, some feats more dramatic than others, some the simple act of maneuvering through a day with self-doubt and uncertainty. The simple trip from front door to mailbox, the Masaya volcano. Thank you, Jesus. Or walking through cancer treatment, each treatment increasing in difficulty, or going to the store in a pandemic with a subpar immune system. Definite flying Wallenda. Yes, there is fear, but faith is the balancing pole that keeps me steady on the beam as I inch over the abyss, as we all keep inching. Please God, thank you God. Thank you for these blessings.

Reflections

Amy Mevorach

This poem was born from the wonder of a news story in combination with a series of poems from my daughter's second grade homework, called "Reverso poems".

Amy Mevorach is a writer in Natick, MA, using quarantine to consider the quality of time over the quantity.

Reflections

Even now
No time is wasted.
NASA ascertained in Antarctica
that high energy particles stream from the ice, a fountain of cosmic light
some newspapers called evidence
of a parallel universe
where laws of physics operate in reverse
and time moves backward.
I always knew this
when confronted –
somewhere the rules are the opposite.
I dwelled in both worlds and committed no loyalties
because I believed in the sphere
of wholeness.

Because I believed in the sphere
I dwelled in both worlds and committed no loyalties.
Somewhere the rules are the opposite
when confronted.
I always knew this...
and time moves backward.
Where laws of physics operate in reverse
of a parallel universe,
some newspapers called evidence
that high energy particles stream from the ice, a fountain of cosmic light
NASA ascertained in Antarctica.
No time was wasted.
Even now.

Infinite Journey

Richard E. Berg

I hope this poem may help someone draw strength, find solace, or otherwise benefit from it.

Richard E. Berg is a Poet and Nature Photographer as well as an Advocate for the Safe Roads Alliance of Massachusetts. He has a deep emotional connection to the poems he writes.

Infinite Journey

Darkness dances between parallel atmospheres
Scattering illuminations of twilight grace the new day
As dawn's first light cascades over the horizon
Meeting me at its shore

This eternal rising
An ever-present sacred energy, calming, focused, restorative
Here, in quiet contemplation, I am by myself, never alone

Life an art-form
An epic voyage of rediscovering the artist as work of art
Weathering the storm, par for the course

Storms-a-brewing, dark clouds in tow
Winds-a-howling, surely you know
A matter of time before a swift lashing rain
Sweeps down hard, with the grip of a chain
No one plans to be there, when you're there
You know it

A turbulent past released from deep in the mansions of your soul
Where dark hearts dispel midnight dreams
Where crying, the ultimate human emotion resides
Where healing becomes wisdom and wisdom becomes strength

The past always pales in comparison to the future
The genius of being

Before the beginning there was nothing
In the beginning there was something
In the end there will again be nothing
In between is everything

Embrace this moment
Because the rest of your life
Is always one hundred percent

© Christine Strickland Photography

"Quite honestly, it was knee jerk reaction for me, my sister and sister-in-law to say yes when I saw it posted on Facebook what seems like a lifetime ago.

In reflecting on it, we're a family, through thick and thin, good times and not so good times, we encourage one another, we jump into help when we feel the need, we hold one another accountable, we share lots of memories and memorable moments, lots of laughs, lots of tears and fears. At the end of the day we love one another and it's the hope we need for the future, it was passed into us and it's up to us to pass it onto the next generation."

~ The Harrington Family ~

Hope

John Ritz

"Hope" is a semi-autobiographical song I have been refining for several decades. It seems to fit our current situation, facing new challenges with so many questions. We'll be okay if we remember there's always hope.

John Ritz is a Hopkinton resident for nearly 30 years. Husband, hiker, musician, pragmatic optimist.

Hope

Young man on the shoreline,
skipping stones on the sea.
He's staring past the horizon,
looking for the sunrise-to-be.
He's waiting for the dawning,
that's bringing on the day.
He's thinking about adventures,
gone with yesterday.

He's singing...

I see everything changing,
I see it every day.
I don't see things staying,
no, nothing stays the same.
And I don't know if I like that.
Don't think I can cope.
Don't know just what to expect.
I only hope there's hope.
I only hope there's hope.

New dad with his baby,
sitting on the sand.
He wonders about the ways this child
will change the dreams he had.
Which new roads will be taken?

Which old paths will be passed?
Will this blue-eyed beginning
be the end of his past?

He's singing...

I see everything changing,
I see it every day.
I don't see things staying,
no, nothing stays the same.
And I don't know if I like that.
Don't think I can cope.
Don't know just what to expect.
I only hope there's hope.
I only hope there's hope.

Old man in the window,
staring out at the bay.
He watches as the tide rolls out,
and takes the day away.
He's got the penthouse office,
successful company.
He's the man with the answers,
still he's questioning the sea.

He's singing...

I see everything changing,
I see it every day.
And I don't see things staying,
no, nothing stays the same.
But I've found that I like that,
and I've found I can cope.
I still don't know just what to expect.
But now I know there's hope.
I've found there's always hope.

Moving Pictures

Nancy Kouchouk

Borders are closing during the Pandemic; we live with fear and loss. In this poem, a foreigner struggles to express himself. By reaching out to another, he finds the courage to tell his story.

While living in the Middle East, Nancy Kouchouk was embraced by a culture whose slow pace was an open palm to hospitality. Dignity for all was preserved in language, and honoring customs and traditions. She writes so that she will never forget.

Moving Pictures

Today I came with train. He coughed dust.
He was sick and mad for stopping.
He dragged rear legs, screeching like dog
for letting people out.

I know in his chest he feels like wrinkled apricot.
In dreams, he wants to be young and lively,
with girls and boys in every window seat.

A train empty is like tree with no leaves.
Tears of his country follow every road he takes.
He must fill with hats, satchels and yippy dog.

A train begins with loud balloons of coming.
His horn celebrates. Inside metal box cars,
people rest and eat. Wheels take them
by hand wherever they want to go.

The sun makes smiles of green.
She laps ground to make shiny grass pool.
At home I step across river rocks like buttons.
Each one opens to kiss my bare feet.

I feel home when I lie on my back.
Sky brings whispering pictures.
Grass talks to me in my born tongue.
I am young juicy apricot.

Come. We don't need metal box train.
I take you to my country. Lie down.
Listen. Let your body ride the grass.

Hope Is Action

Carolyn Waters

I wrote this submission against a backdrop of civil unrest and upheaval taking place in this country and around the world. People protesting for change as men and women, African Americans, die in the streets, on the sidewalks and in their homes. I see hope in this unrest, people standing up and trying to change the world from what it is to what it could be. But these folks need help, they can't do it alone. Like those who have come before us, those who have forged change, we can't be bystanders, we have to operationalize hope. In my submission, I ask how you will make the things you hope for become a reality.

Carolyn Waters is a performing singing/songwriter based in Worcester, MA. Her style, described as "socially conscious soul", reflects her deep connection and love for all things music as well as her commitment to use music and the arts as a tool to promote healing and positive social change. As a songwriter her original music not only looks to support and encourage, but also challenges people to actively examine and change the world in which they live.

Hope Is Action

Hope is defined as *a feeling of expectation and desire for a certain thing to happen, to want something to happen or to be the case.* I think we all can remember doing it, hoping for that special something: that new bike for Christmas, that someone will ask you to that big dance, that we wouldn't be the last one to be picked for the kickball team. Hope served us well as children, in our small, isolated, protected world (for most of us). But as we grow older and really start to live our lives on a higher level of consciousness, we observe a world filled with prejudices, inequality, social and economic injustices and we begin to redefine what hope is. Redefining it to a definition that doesn't tell us to want, to wish, to wait, but to one that tells us to stand, to walk, to march and scream and protest for the things we want to see, for equality, for justice, for people just like and unlike ourselves.

From marches in Selma, sleep-in's for Occupy Wall Street to Black Lives Matter, we see this new bigger definition in action, *hope that incorporates action,* which tells us if we *want a certain thing to happen,* we need to get up and make it happen. Through fire hoses, attack dogs, tear gas to rubber bullets; from the shouts of 'we shall overcome', calls for people to make good trouble, necessary trouble, to cries of 'I can't breathe' we have seen and continue to see thousands of people (young, old, black, white, brown) taking to the streets, actively trying to change the world for the better. So, whatever your cause, whatever you 'hope' for, stand, walk, vote, march, scream, and protest. The world is waiting!

If love is what you need, sow the seeds, sow the seeds
If love is what you need, sow the seeds, sow the seeds
Grab the love in your soul
It will tell you where to go
If love, love, love is what you need
Then let it grow, let it grow

If joy is what you need, then sing your song, sing your song
If joy is what you need, then sing your song, sing your song
Sing out loud, sing out strong
Show the world your inner song
If joy, joy, joy is what you need
Then sing your song, sing your song

If understanding is what you need then shake a hand, shake a hand
If understanding is what you need shake a hand, shake a hand
Reach a hand across that isle
Put on those shoes, walk that mile
If under-stand-stand-ding is what you need
Then walk that mile. Walk that mile

If hope is what you need then don't stand down, don't stand down
If hope is what you need then don't stand down, don't stand down
Wear your heart on your sleeve, don't sit down, take a knee
If hope, hope, hope is what you need
Then don't stand down, don't stand down

From "Give What You Need" Song Lyrics written by Carolyn Waters,
copyright, 2019

How to Heal Our Community

Teresa Mei Chuc

I wrote this poem because during this challenging time of closures and quarantine due to COVID-19, we need each other and mutual aid more than ever. When people are losing their jobs, unable to pay rent and unable to get food to feed themselves and their families, we realize how the current colonial system based on capitalism, competition and individualism that benefit the privileged doesn't serve those most in need and how much we need our community ... trading and sharing resources, supporting each other. This is how we can survive.

Former Poet Laureate of Altadena, California (2018 to 2020), Teresa Mei Chuc is the author of three full-length collections of poetry, *Red Thread* (Fithian Press, 2012), *Keeper of the Winds* (FootHills Publishing, 2014) and *Invisible Light* (Many Voices Press, 2018). She was born in Saigon, Vietnam and immigrated to the U.S. under political asylum with her mother and brother shortly after the Vietnam War while her father remained in a Vietcong "reeducation" camp for nine years. Teresa is a graduate of the Masters in Fine Arts in Creative Writing program (Poetry) at Goddard College in Plainfield, Vermont and teaches literature and writing at a public high school in Los Angeles.

How to Heal Our Community

If only we could operate
the way mushrooms do.
Their mycelium transporting
resources, nutrients
and messages
to where they are needed
through multiple possible
pathways, in case any
get disrupted, to help
the plant grow and thrive.

Pandemic

BJ Feeney

I wrote this poem as I feel the pandemic has become a new learning curve for mankind, a global voice for change if we are to continue our existence here on planet Earth. The "pause" has forced us to face ourselves and become more grateful for what we already have, and to create a more compassionate type of thinking towards one another. It has given me a stronger feeling of hope for humanity.

BJ Feeney is a retired reading/writing instructor, now focused on publishing her own projects across genres. She recently published a spiritual self-help book entitled, *Gabriel's Light: Spiritual Poetic Musings* (Balboa Press), and is featured in a children's poetry anthology about preservation of the sea to be published this fall. She is an active member of The Writers' Loft in Sherborn, MA. Currently she is working on picture books and illustrated short stories.

Pandemic

A sacred time of renewal
No barriers of thought
No closed doors to will

Stillness rises
Greeting day's opening
Gratitude immeasurable

Compassion rules
Newsrooms notice bravery
Goodness arrives unannounced

We live inside one another
Terrified, yet hopeful
Curved into one another's eyes

Connections stronger
Constant pulsating drumbeats
Upon Earth's door

Our small light specks
become blindingly real
when blended as One

The spiral of hope
Will get us through
Coming full circle

Mankind has been here
in another time of woe
Bent upon learning about itself

© Chelsea Bradway

"The silver lining of this pandemic has been the bonus time spent with our grown children. It's been an adventure relearning to live together under the same roof and so much fun creating more memories in our family home."

~ Kate Higgins Wraight ~

In Answer

Doreen LeBlanc

My poem was a reaction to a friend who was feeling quite overwhelmed and helpless during the first few difficult days of April and wondered what was his purpose.

Doreen LeBlanc lives in Massachusetts, is a practitioner of Jin Shin Jyutsu, energy balancing, and spends several months at her cabin in Cape Breton, Nova Scotia, where she was born. Inspiration bubbles up out of the river and sea, streams down the mountain, and comes through family stories and the beauty of Cape Breton and her Acadian and Scottish heritage.

In Answer

Ahh you ask me the big question of the ages
You are here to exhale
To smile
To be
Thought-full, compassionate
To find purpose in being human
To be the bell ringer
Protester of injustice
Protector of Mother Earth
Appreciator of magnolias in spring
This world needs more caring uncles
Kind, supportive neighbors
Music makers
You

© Lynne Damianos

"We participated in The Front Steps Project to support Amazing Things Arts Center. There is a strong arts community in MetroWest, but they need our help during difficult days. It is also important to mark and record this point in time. We staged this picture to represent how we are spending our time being homebound. Reading, on computers or screens, caring for our new doggie – very typical of most families during COVID-19 2020."

~ The Cerutti-Harris Family ~

Pandemic

Carol Esler

By the time this is published, I will be a 70 years old woman. I write because putting words together well is a healing activity.

Carol Esler is a retired social worker, a Hopkinton resident for many decades and a person finding much contentment in friendship and creativity.

Pandemic

The last of the snowflakes swirl outside
as we begin to realize
that this change
will not be small
or short
or easy
It is a portal
like between seasons
when we must
neither yearn for what was
or what will be
Do work for the good
the fair
the truth
and our grandchildren
We endure
finding new ways of being
of pacing our tasks
And learning
and loving
and being
under this gray and shining sky

© Chelsea Bradway

"When we purchased our home from the Beals, we vowed to be positive and present community members and uphold the sense of belonging and giving back that the Beals family and home had instilled for so many years. When the uprising for a (continued) revolution against racism and brutality towards People of Color and the kind was drawn in the sand between "Black/Brown and Blue", we knew exactly what our calling was for our community and beyond. We, a mixed-race, multi-ethnic, police supporting family, would bridge the gap and show support for those who vow to protect us while raising our voices for those who look and fear like us and telling our truths to those who may not. Our goal was to show our strength and our vulnerability."

~ Lana Dugale ~

The Welcoming Dance

Cheryl Perreault

I decided to write about one of the best moments in my life when I danced with a perfect stranger. Despite all the division and afflictions we have been facing, this joyful woman and welcoming neighborhood gave me a memory of possibility and hope for all the world to feel more often, the important joy of our interconnection.

Cheryl Perreault has a background in Psychology and is a spoken-word artist. She has two cd recordings of original poetry accompanied by the guitar music of Steve Rapson. She has worked as an educator with people of all ages and with hospice patients writing their stories of life in review. Cheryl has also hosted programs of poetry, story and song for community and HCAM-TV and is co-editor with Cynthia Franca of two anthologies of poetry and stories written by people of our "world house." Since the pandemic, she has taken to sitting very still in her yard to listen and applaud the poetry, stories and songs of nearby birds, squirrels and trees.

The Welcoming Dance

In the summer of 2019, my husband and I were visiting our daughter in her D.C. neighborhood, where welcoming signs hung from doorways and rainbow flags waved for the Pride Parade that had been taking place that weekend. People would look at you and smile, even ask your name. There were people walking all sizes of smiling dogs, and at one point, a teacher led a chain of small children gripping one long rope across the street, making everyone smile.

As we were sitting at the outdoor patio of a café, a car stopped in the street just a few feet from our table emitting loud, pulsating music from the radio. The passenger door opened and an elegant woman wearing a sleeveless, flowing dress with short, buzz-cut hair and tattooed arms adorned by jingling, silver bangle bracelets stepped out and began dancing in the middle of the street, causing the café spectators to smile and some to stand as they watched her dance in ecstatic, unbridled joy.

At that moment, a police car pulled up behind her and slowed down. We watched, wondering how she could possibly be reprimanded—simply for dancing out so much joy?

But no such thing in this love-minded neighborhood as this rapturous woman simply danced to one side, leaving enough room for the car to proceed. There was a collective sigh of relief as the patrol car drove by. The officer seemed to be smiling.

Then this ambassador of dance noticed us. I almost knew what she was thinking as she looked us over and began to dance her way over to our table. Although my husband and daughter were saying "no thank you" in their minds, I was silently shouting "YES!" in mine. Sure enough, she seemed to have heard as she held her arms out to me to dance. How could I not?

 It was, in that moment, an instant state of bliss and an ecstatic celebration of life dance. We were women of different shades of skin; one of us had tattoos, one of us had arms unadorned. We didn't know a thing about each other's lives, but it was as if we were of one body and it was at once, fun, funny, sanctifying, and sacred to share this joy of such a moment of deep, felt interconnection.

We hugged and she danced away back to her car. In retrospect, I can't remember any of the details, just the pure, sudden energy of it. I loved that moment of dancing with a perfect stranger. I loved that wonderful dancing woman. I loved the officer in the patrol car, and I loved the smiling people at the café.

Furthermore, I loved the great privilege of being alive in that moment, dancing and feeling momentary interconnection with everyone and everything.

I wish more of these moments for all people of our world.

I wish us all more moments of feeling love for one another and for honoring together the precious gift of breath and dance, and life.

You Have the Key

Hyppolite Ntigurirwa

I offer the poem from my belief that Peace is What You Give, Not What You Ask Others to Give You". The key for Joy, Hope and Peace for the world to be a much better place is only held by one person – YOU.

Hyppolite Ntigurirwa is a 2020 Postgraduate World Fellow at Yale University. He is artist, activist, and founder of Be the Peace, an organization focusing on the use of art to halt the intergenerational transmission of hate and to promote the power of cross-generational healing. A child survivor of the 1994 genocide against the Tutsi, Hyppolite continues to promote reconciliation and peace throughout Rwanda. In 2019, he envisioned and conducted the "Be the Peace Walk," a 100-day performance piece in which he walked across the country in commemoration of 25 years since the end of the genocide. Hyppolite was an international Artist-in-Residence with Arts Connect International in Boston in 2016. Since then, he has worked as Arts Program Manager for the British Council in Rwanda, focused on disability rights and societal inclusion. He is a Peace Ambassador for One Young World, Peace Scholar and his work has been covered by global media including BBC, NPR, SABC, and Dutchwelle. Hyppolite's famous quote is: ***"Peace Is What You Give, Not What You Ask Others To Give You"***.

You Have the Key…

This key I choose will help unlock the suffering caused by starvation, wars, suicide, revenge, anger, relationships, money, jobs, position, nationalité, sex, ubumuga, beauty, impano, our belongings, umuco, habits, culture, imitungo…

I hold this key and share this key
because it is the key of remembering
that all together we can find a way

A way to peace   A way to love
A way to forgive A way to confess,
A way to help the oppressed
A way to lift each other
There is a way.

Always when you are holding this key
you will remember when
not only in the past

but remember when
in the present
in the future

Remember
you are not alone,

you have your key,
for liberating the self,

a key for mystery,
for hope,
for miracles,

Urufunguzo rw'amayobera,
rw'ibyiza, rw'urukundo,
rw'umutuzo n'amahoro...

This key is not only for you,
but also for your neighbour,

not only for your life
but also for others' lives

There is a way and
we can find that way
for we are one people,
we have the key
in our hands
in our hearts
in our spirits
right now.

*Editor's note: some words of Hyppolite's poem were written in Kinyarwanda, the national language of Rwanda, and the first language of the entire population of the country. It is one of the country's official languages alongside French, English, and Swahili.

About the Photographers

Chelsea Bradway

When school ended abruptly in March, I found myself searching for some structure with a dash of whimsy. I saw a post about Carla Soulia and her photography project (#thefrontstepsproject). I was intrigued and excited about the possibility of bringing some fun and whimsy to my little town of Southborough. I spent the next couple of weeks laughing and smiling with my community while taking pictures on their front steps. The added bonus was that we were able to raise over $15,000 for the Southborough Food Pantry and Southborough Youth and Family Services. I have always wanted to be able to give back and this was a fun and beautiful way to bring some joy to the town.

Chelsea Bradway is a New England photographer who creates magic in the ordinary by bringing together people, places, and props in unconventional poses and settings. The results are hauntingly beautiful black and white and color photographs that can be simultaneously innocent, beautiful, and dark. Born in the Berkshires, Chelsea is an explorer who is constantly challenging herself with new surroundings and experiences and brings a sense of adventure to all that she does. Chelsea teaches photography to children, relishing their remarkable and daring creativity and gives them a safe outlet behind their cameras. Chelsea, who has a Masters Degree from Simmons College in Education/ Intensive Special Needs, has shown her work regionally and internationally, including at Fountain Street Gallery in Boston, Gallery X in New Bedford, Plymouth Center for the Arts in Plymouth and The Julia Margaret Cameron Award Exhibition for Women Photographers in Barcelona, Spain. Website: https://www.allthingssparkley.com

Lynne Damianos

As a full-time commercial photographer, I typically spend my time creating images of architecture, people and products for business. During the pandemic Stay at Home Advisory, I wanted to celebrate connection and bring people together who might feel isolated. I aimed to highlight the faces of our community during a time when we might not see them in passing. I photographed 5-minute portraits of 70 Framingham families at a safe distance in front of their homes between April 11 and May 9, 2020 and requested donations to keep the arts alive at ātac (Amazing Things Arts Center) in downtown Framingham. The experience was profoundly heartwarming to me and to the participants (most donated to ātac although they had not even been there yet, because the arts are so important to them). The beautiful people that I photographed uplifted me, and this project provided a bit of joy to all of us amid the uncertainty of the day.

Lynne provides distinctive photography of the built environment, products/artwork, and people for business. She believes that photography is a collaborative process with her clients and takes details seriously. Photography is her passion. Lynne is an active educator, presenting a wide variety of custom photography and Photoshop seminars designed for professionals and students. She is a faculty member of Keefe at Night and Tri-County Continuing Education Program. She was an Artist-in-Residence at both Holliston & Framingham, MA High Schools as part of an Integration Technology Grant from the Massachusetts Department of Education titled "Capturing Architecture Past and Present." She continues to add to her series of personal *NatureScapes* and *BuildingScapes* images, which have been exhibited in a variety of group and solo shows. She also enjoys kayaking, yoga, hiking and hand bell ringing ("bell therapy").
Website: www.DamianosPhotography.com

Christine Strickland

When asked about my experience photographing families in this challenging time my response was, "Ever since I can remember, I have always looked for the silver lining in any situation, good or bad; the Coronavirus Pandemic wasn't any different to me. Through my involvement with the Front Step Project, my silver lining takeaway is that while my photography business ground to a complete stop, I cherished my time with the project as I met so many new families that I ordinarily wouldn't have had the opportunity to meet had it not been for COVID-19. I got involved with this wonderful project as it allowed me to give families a reason to shower, get dressed, smile and have fun while raising almost $15,000 in donations, in lieu of payment to me, for Hopkinton's Project Just Because.

Christine Strickland is the owner of Christine Strickland Photography in Hopkinton, MA. Her love-affair with photography began in 1977 when she was in the 5th grade. Her Nana allowed her to borrow her camera when her class took a week-long field trip and that was it … she became hooked on taking photos. Vacations with her husband and the birth of their three daughters, along with the introduction of digital technology, continued to solidify her love for this hobby. After 26 years in Corporate America, she was given the opportunity to pursue her dream of starting her own photography business. As the owner of Christine Strickland Photography, she looks forward to meeting new people and families every day. She thoroughly enjoys taking portrait headshots for rising high school seniors and as well as shooting professional headshots.
Website: https://christinestricklandphotography.com/